Brought to you by

SANTA CLARA COUNTY

4000 Moorpark Ave., Suite 200
San Jose, CA 95117
P 408.260.3700
F 408.296.5642

www.first5kids.org

The First 5 years.
Make them count.

HOW TO RAISE EMOTIONALLY HEALTHY CHILDREN

Meeting the Five Critical Needs of Children . . . And Parents Too!

GERALD NEWMARK, Ph.D.

NMI Publishers
Tarzana, California

NOTE

In this book, we avoid the awkward locutions he/she, him/her. We generally use the more traditional male pronouns which present less stylistic difficulty. The reader should understand that *she* could be substituted for *he* in most instances when it is used in this text to refer to a non-gender noun such as *child*. The same is true of *he* substituting for *she* whenever the latter is used in the same context.

Second Edition
First Printing

Published by
NMI Publishers
18653 Ventura Boulevard, Suite 547
Tarzana, CA 91356
(818) 708-1244
nmipub@earthlink.net
www.emotionallyhealthychildren.com

Cover Design: Steve Gussman
Cover Photo: Alex Jauregui
Book Design: Tina Hill

Library of Congress Control Number: 2007905877

ISBN: 978-0-932767-13-4

Printed in the United States of America

To my wonderful wife,
Deborah,
who wakes up smiling,
goes to sleep smiling, and
fills my life with
pride and joy.

Contents

Foreword

With the multitude of books on parenting and child-rearing already at hand, it is both surprising and refreshing to welcome a new one marked by a straightforward and intelligible approach that is as relevant for adults as for the children it addresses. Dr. Newmark challenges the time-honored, emotion-driven, "seat-of-the-pants" approach to parenting, and suggests instead that parents use an intentional, systematized strategy that recognizes and responds to five critical needs of kids. These emotional needs—to feel respected, to feel important, to feel accepted, to feel included, and to feel secure—are neither obscure nor hard to understand. Their importance is obvious. They clearly contribute to self-esteem and self-worth. Yet, as the author abundantly shows, parents' emotional or erratic responses often deny these needs, leaving an accumulating residue of anxiety, self-doubt, and uncertainty in the mind of the child.

What is more, these needs are just as important to adults. Unfortunately, in our interactions with each other, they are too often ignored to the detriment of our personal relationships and our own mental health. Can we possibly learn better from our children? It is fitting that Dr. Newmark repeatedly suggests that our children have something to teach us if we will but watch and listen. They frequently have ideas we fail to see as relevant or useful, and express truths that escape us.

This is a book that parents—especially new parents—should have by their bedside. It is a book that child agency personnel and professional caregivers should read and recommend to their clients and patients. Its simple message is one that youth workers should incorporate in their work and that teachers should apply in their classrooms. I think parents (and other adults) who successfully practice meeting these critical needs in their children will certainly raise emotionally healthier kids, and as a secondary benefit, hardly less important, significantly improve their own mental health.

Roy W. Menninger, M.D.
Menninger Foundation

Preface

A Wake-Up Call for America: The Missing Agenda

After publication of the first edition of *How to Raise Emotionally Healthy Children,* I spoke to about 100 people on "The Neglect of the Emotional Health of Our Children: A National Problem." I received a standing ovation when I finished. As I autographed books afterward, my grown-up son, David, was at the other end of the same table selling them. He had not yet read the book, and this was the first time he had ever heard me speak publicly.

A woman who was purchasing a book started chatting with David. Given the warm reception I had received from the audience, I was curious what he might be saying to the lady, so I eavesdropped and heard her inquire, "What's your relationship with Dr. Newmark?" My son replied "Oh, he's my father." She then asked, "What's it like having a father who wrote a book titled, *How to Raise Emotionally Healthy Children?*" David replied instantly, "I wish he knew that stuff when I was growing up!"

She laughed. I stood up, moved nearer to David, and exclaimed, "David, I wish I had known 'that stuff' when you were growing up." Actually, I wish my parents had known "that stuff" and their parents, too. We just didn't know there was anything to know. The truth is that, along with most parents, we were all victims of our ignorance.

The story of how and why I came to write this book is the story of how I became a child advocate. I was born into a poor family in Bronx, New York, was accepted to college on probation, dropped out after two years, and was drafted into the army. For too many years, my life was intermittently filled with fear, depression, and despair. Fortunately, along the way I met the right people at the right time. They helped me gain enough confidence and knowledge to achieve emotional, educational, and career success. Helping others—especially young people—became a driving force throughout my life as a teacher, consultant, and researcher.

As my formal career ended, my interest in parent-child relations and school problems increased. Looking deeper into the causes of these problems, I found it ironic and troubling that most problems facing contemporary societies were, and still are, people problems, not technical problems; yet we paid little or no attention to human relations and emotional health and the same is true today. We know how to send people into space and produce incredible advances in science, electronics, and medicine. However, when it comes to living peacefully and treating one another in emotionally healthy ways, we seem to be at a loss.

This disparity is especially serious for children because their emotional needs are neglected both at home and at school. Only in a crisis do a child's emotional needs receive attention. After an incident of school violence, or a tragedy such as September 11, countless human-relations professionals arrive at schools to explore children's feelings and emotions and to counsel and comfort them. A few weeks later it is business as usual, and their emotional needs are rarely addressed again. I call this the "missing agenda."

The missing agenda adversely affects millions of children, the so-called "at risk" kids, who go through their school years anxious, confused, angry, isolated, moody, sad, or depressed. Substantial numbers of these children become school failures and dropouts who turn to sex, crime, drugs, gangs, and violence as outlets for their unhappiness and rage.

A much larger group are the millions of kids, academically successful and apparently trouble-free, who have similar fears, concerns, and problems that are rarely expressed and that go unnoticed by parents or teachers. These children carry their emotional insecurities, hang-ups, and scars into adulthood, causing them to become insecure, unhappy, misguided, or troubled adults who make up the statistics of divorce, drug abuse, suicide, crime, depression, and other emotional problems. These inadequacies frequently are passed on from parent to child, one generation to the next, and include all socioeconomic groups.

I wrote *How to Raise Emotionally Healthy Children* to raise public consciousness about the problem and to provide a practical resource to enable parents and teachers to create emotionally healthy environments for kids and themselves. In the book, I identify five critical needs that all children have throughout their lives—*the need to feel respected, important, accepted, included, and secure.* Satisfying these needs provides a foundation for developing self-confident, independent, thinking, caring, civic-minded individuals, with greater prospects for success in school, career, marriage, and life in general.

Following the book's publication, I spoke to hundreds of people and soon realized that there was a hunger for this information. People felt we were talking about them. They identified with the content and felt they already knew it, without having known that they knew it. Inspired by the enthusiasm from people of widely different backgrounds, the mission became to get the book to as many adults as possible who influence children. To accomplish this, the decision was to sell the book at a price so low that nobody would be denied a book because of cost.

Together with my wife, Deborah, we initiated *The Children's Project*—a non-commercial effort to spread our message to parents, educators, childcare providers, and policymakers and, at the same time, focus on developing special programs for schools and cities.

The success of the book has been astonishing and gratifying. The sale of more than 250,000 copies has been accomplished without any publicity—strictly through word-of-mouth. About 50 percent of the books have been purchased by schools (pre-school, K-12, and colleges) for distribution to parents, teachers, and some high school and college students.

The other 50 percent of the books have been distributed to childcare provider and child advocacy institutions, including peri- and prenatal departments of hospitals, child-abuse prevention organizations, and community parent-education programs. One perinatal institution purchased 60,000 books and is distributing them to 19 hospitals, where they are given to parents of newborn infants and used in parenting classes.

The success of both the English and Spanish editions in the United States, across diverse ethnic, socioeconomic, religious, and age groups, and the worldwide interest indicated by translations in Mexico, Hungary, Israel, and soon Russia, has stimulated us to set ambitious goals. With this 2nd edition, we present an expanded vision of how parents can satisfy children's emotional needs at home, while teachers satisfy these same needs in every classroom throughout a child's school years. In this way, we envisage creating emotional-health-friendly schools which can have a significant impact on a child's academic, social, and civic development.

With the popularity of the book, and the low price at which we make it available, we feel there is no limit to the number of people, schools, and childcare organizations we can reach. In a world traumatized by strife and war, we feel blessed to have a message and a resource that can bring people together and enrich their lives. By creating a positive atmosphere in which people interact with people in ways that make everyone feel *respected, important, accepted, included,* and *secure,* we can become a powerful force for developing emotionally healthy and high-achieving children, families, and schools—our own and those of others. And, who knows? If enough of us get involved, we might just change the world.

Gerald Newmark, Ph.D.

Introduction

(Challenges of Parenting: Pleasures, Paradoxes, Pitfalls)

*A*s a parent, what a joy it was to wake up in the morning feeling confident that all interactions with my child would be positive and rewarding; that I knew what was needed to develop an emotionally healthy child and how to provide it; that no matter what came up during the day, my behavior would be consistent and positive, and that I would rarely feel overwhelmed, frustrated, out-of-control, or at a loss to know what to do.

Further, what a pleasure it was to go to sleep knowing that most of the time I had done the right things that day, and I had little or no anxiety or guilt about anything. It was also reassuring to know that if my behavior was "off," I'd be able to recognize it quickly and take corrective action.

How fortunate, too, that my wife and I were in agreement about parenting philosophy and practices and that we would discuss how we were doing on a regular basis, not just when some problem arose. We felt good not to be passive parents, waiting to react to things that went wrong or to problem situations, but rather to be proactively creating a cohesive, happy, dynamic family life. We also realized how wonderful it was for our child to have parents who were relaxed and confident, and who appeared to know what they were doing.

If the above sounds to you like a dream, you are right. That's not the way it was for us, nor is it like that for most parents. For most of us, along with the joy and excitement of parenting, there is much anxiety, insecurity, and inconsistency. Like so many others, our approach to parenting was random, unfocused, and crisis-oriented. Any idea of what parenting could be like at its best or of a thoughtful, systematic approach was unfamiliar to us. As my knowledge, experience, and expertise in parent-child relations grew, so did the idea for this book—the notion being to prepare a blueprint that would help parents make the dream described above become a reality. The following thoughts are presented as an introduction to the themes of this book.

Being a parent is one of the greatest joys that one experiences in life, but it's also one of the most difficult and anxiety-provoking responsibilities any of us will ever have. It is among the most important, challenging, and complex tasks a human being has in a lifetime, yet we come to it almost totally unprepared, with little or no training. It is also apparent that once one is a parent, one is a parent forever, and frequently it doesn't get easier over time. I remember my mother saying, "When the kids were little, we had little problems. When they were big, we had big problems." Parents never stop worrying about their children, no matter how old they are, and rarely stop treating them as children, even after they become adults.

Today, our children are growing up in an age of anxiety, change, and uncertainty—one which is probably more difficult for children than any previous time in history. As an example of this uncertainty, high school students today face the probability of having to change jobs or careers at least three or four times in their lifetime, and many of these do not exist at present. We are frightened by the number and seriousness of teenage problems such as suicides and attempted suicides, alcohol and drug abuse, cigarette smoking, sexual promiscuity, school dropouts, crime, and violence. And many of these problems now occur during pre-teen years.

Our fears and worries often interfere with giving children what they need. Frequently, we try too hard to protect them and to mold them. We talk, we preach, we scold, we punish, we lecture, we give advice. One minute we threaten them, and the next we shower them with love.

Too often, parents are reactive rather than proactive, correcting something the child has done, rather than consciously striving to create a positive environment where praise and encouragement outweigh correction. We lack a vision of what parenting could be like at its best and a strategy for achieving it.

The context in which all this takes place is not one where there is a dearth of information on parenting. On the contrary, there is a wealth of information—perhaps even an overabundance—and it is often contradictory. At times, parents are overwhelmed with too much to assimilate and no overall philosophy or tools to help translate concepts into everyday actions beneficial to children.

Being a parent is not something that you learn once and master for all time. We are not naturally skilled or emotionally prepared for parenting, nor do we automatically get better with experience. When we add to this the constant changes occurring in society, it becomes clear that parents are faced with the challenge of being active, lifelong learners.

My basic thesis is that all children have five critical needs that are essential to their emotional health. These are the need to feel *respected, important, accepted, included,* and *secure.* When parents understand these five basic needs, recognize their importance, and become knowledgeable as to how to satisfy them, they can develop an effective, overall strategy and a consistent approach to parenting. In so doing, there is an increased likelihood of our becoming the parents we might want to be: proactive rather than reactive, appropriately protective rather than overly controlling or permissive, affirming rather than negative, consistent rather than haphazard, relaxed rather than tense.

Within this framework, parents will start to master the art of giving children enough freedom so they can grow in their ability to make decisions and become self-confident, independent, responsible, thinking, caring, civic-minded people. At the same time, they will be able to provide sufficient structure, guidance, and discipline so children don't harm themselves or grow into self-indulgent, inconsiderate, non-civic-minded individuals.

This book presents a philosophy of parenting and an action-oriented strategy, based on the five critical needs of children, that is designed to achieve emotionally healthy children, parents, and families. This is accomplished by:

◆ Presenting a vision of what parenting can be at its best: purposeful, systematic, proactive, consistent, self-correcting, inclusive, positive.

◆ Providing a philosophy of parenting—a set of core values—that enables parents to interact with children from a sense of conviction and strength.

◆ Focusing on the five critical needs of children that contribute significantly to their emotional health, and specifying the methods by which parents can satisfy these needs.

◆ Explaining why common sense and love are necessary and important, but not sufficient, and defining love in a way that makes it a more meaningful force in parenting.

◆ Spelling out a strategy that empowers parents to act confidently and consistently in ways that are less stressful and more rewarding to parents and children.

◆ Providing specific action plans that help even the busiest parents engage in growth experiences with their children and create balanced lifestyles for themselves.

◆ Giving parents simple but powerful tools to measure their effectiveness and make constructive and timely changes.

Children who grow up with this kind of parenting are more likely to:

◆ Have self-respect and interact with parents and others respectfully.

◆ Feel important and be able to relate to people and situations with confidence.

◆ Accept themselves and others and have a positive outlook on life.

◆ Welcome responsibilities and tasks that enhance family living.

◆ Become self-reliant and able to resist negative influences from peers and society.

◆ Acquire self-discipline and avoid impulsive, self-destructive actions.

◆ Openly share joys, anxieties, and problems with parents and be willing to seek information and advice from them.

◆ Be secure enough to listen to criticism, admit faults, and make changes.

◆ Build positive relations with siblings and peers.

To write this book, I have relied on several sources. Initial concepts came from my personal experience, analyzing relations, and interactions as a child with my own parents and as a parent with my own child, and as a teacher with my students and their parents. From these initial reflections, I began to formulate some general ideas and many questions about the needs of children and behavior of parents which thwarted or satisfied these needs.

These ideas started to coalesce during the seven years I was co-director of a Ford Foundation-supported project to create a model elementary school in the Los Angeles City Schools. In working closely with teachers, parents, and children, it became apparent that some adults were more effective with children than others. Seeking to find out what accounted for these differences, I started to observe parent-child interactions more closely, followed by extended conversations with parents, teachers, and children. At this stage, my concept of the five critical needs of children began to crystallize.

Out of this, I developed a series of lectures and seminars on parent-child relations which were sponsored by school, religious, and civic groups. Confirmation of the concept of the five critical needs of children emerged from interviews with, and questionnaires completed by, several hundred young people and parents attending these sessions. The material and conclusions presented here represent a synthesis of these experiences and a lifetime of observation and study.

This book was written for parents of children of all ages and expectant parents, too. It also has special significance for teachers and schools, for high school and college students, and for all others involved in the well-being of children and families, including policymakers. At its core, it is about enhancing the emotional health of children and parents, strengthening families and schools, about moving rapidly and thoughtfully from concepts to action, and about positive, pleasurable, parenting. It's about parenting as though children *really* matter! And parents, too! Ultimately, it's about creating a better world—one child, one family, one society at a time.

The Five Critical Needs of Children

(Parenting as Though Children Really Matter)

ll children, at all ages, have five critical needs in common which stay with them throughout their lives—the need to feel *respected, important, accepted, included,* and *secure.* I call these needs critical because when satisfied, they are the key to developing an emotionally healthy child. This knowledge serves parents as a roadmap to guide their actions in creating an emotionally healthy home environment. In this chapter, you will learn how parents unknowingly and unintentionally fail to meet their children's emotional needs and the kinds of problems created for children and families. More important, you will find out how parents succeed in creating an emotionally healthy parent-child relationship and the lifetime benefits that accrue. Further, it will become apparent that opportunities to contribute to this daily are within the reach and capability of every parent.

Need to Feel Respected

Children need to feel respected. For that to happen, they need to be treated in a courteous, thoughtful, attentive, and civil manner—as individuals, deserving of the same courtesy and consideration as others. When I was growing up, I repeatedly heard, "Treat your parents with respect—and your teachers and older people too." That's fine, we need to say these things, but one of the best ways for children to learn about respect is to feel what it's like to be treated respectfully and to observe their parents and other adults treating one another the same way.

When children are not treated with respect, it can lower their self-esteem and cause them to become rebellious and to act disrespectfully toward others. It is curious how many parents treat their children in ways they objected to when they were children. In spite of parents apparently knowing better, their early childhood conditioning seems hard to overcome. Children need to be treated with the respect that we ourselves would welcome. For example, it is just as easy and takes the same amount of time to say, "I'm sorry honey. I don't have time right now," rather than "Can't you see I'm busy? Stop bothering me!" With children, a simple act of courtesy can go a long way.

Parents' opinions, values, attitudes, and actions, matter to children, even to teenagers who sometimes pretend not to care. Discourtesy, rudeness, and inconsiderateness on the part of adults is often the result of being thoughtless. We don't think of children as having the same needs as adults, and we do not realize the effect we have on them by what we say and how we say it. When children are treated with respect, they are more likely to act respectfully toward others, including their own children when they become parents.

The following are some examples which indicate considerable room for improvement.

RUDENESS, DISCOURTESY

While visiting a friend who was having a conversation with his eight-year-old son, the telephone rang. Although the child was speaking, the father abruptly got up and without saying a word took the call, engaging the caller in a lengthy conversation. When the child approached and tried to finish what he had been saying, the father frowned and said in a loud voice, "Don't be rude. Can't you see I'm talking?" Now I ask you, "Who was being rude—the father or the son?"

Upon hearing the phone ring, how would it have been if the father had said to his son, "Excuse me, Bobby. Let me see who that is. I'll be right back." And what if he had said to the caller, "I'm sorry, I'll have to call you back. I'm having a conversation with my son." Not only would that have been respectful, but think how important the child might have felt.

One day, while working for a research corporation, my work wasn't going well. Discouraged, I left work early. When I arrived home and walked into the kitchen, my son was already home from school. He was having corn flakes and milk, and I noticed the refrigerator door had been left slightly open. I started scolding him for being thoughtless, and how all the food in the refrigerator would spoil, and how we couldn't afford that kind of waste. Suddenly, David started to cry.

"What are you crying about?" I shouted.

"I didn't do it on purpose; you act like I'm some sort of criminal," he replied.

"What a big baby!" I exclaimed, and left the house.

I took a short walk to calm down, and realized that my reaction was out of proportion to what he had done and that it really had nothing to do with either my son or the refrigerator. It had to do with the way I was feeling about myself and how my work was going. I was acting as though the last thing this kid did, every night before he went to sleep, was to make a list—"How Many Ways Can I Make My Father Miserable Tomorrow." Of course, that was not the case, but my tone of voice and entire manner implied that he had committed a serious offense.

LYING

Another way in which we don't treat children with respect is by lying to them. When we lie to children, we lose credibility. We give them the impression that lying is OK, that maybe adults do not feel they have to be truthful with children. Lying diminishes trust, causing communication to decline, which then creates a further erosion of trust.

Lying starts with seemingly small, insignificant things such as having someone say that you are not at home when you really are or telling a child, "This is for your own good," when we know that it's for our own convenience, or when we make a promise that we don't expect to keep. By so doing, we lose the opportunity to help children gain insights into lying and ethical behavior. And later, when we punish them for lying, we compound the problem.

One newspaper described the extent of the problem by stating that lying had become so prevalent in American society that people frequently don't know when they are lying or telling the truth anymore. For children who want to believe their parents are virtuous, and yet see through some of their lies and hypocrisy, the inner tension has to be troubling. It is frequently disturbing when, as we get older, we realize that our parents are fallible human beings with numerous shortcomings. With children especially, honesty is still the best policy.

DEMEANING BEHAVIOR

When children make mistakes or don't do what we expect of them, and we call them names (bad, dumb, slob, stubborn, lazy, greedy, selfish), or otherwise belittle them by word, tone, or action, we are acting disrespectfully. When I was growing up there was a saying, "Sticks and stones will break your bones, but names will never hurt you." Don't believe it. Names hurt and can make a negative imprint on children, often lasting into adulthood.

Exaggerated anger, impatience, or sarcasm creates defensiveness or retaliatory behavior by the child, and little learning takes place, either by parent or child. For example, to say sarcastically to an 11th grader, who is not showing enough interest in school to satisfy you, that he should look for a job washing dishes, "because that's all you'll be good for if you don't go to college," is both counterproductive and disrespectful. To tell a teenager that her lipstick and dress make her look like a tramp will not encourage her to use you as a consultant on personal grooming. There are respectful ways to address these issues without damaging the relationship and making communication more difficult.

One day while walking around a lake at a neighborhood park, I noticed a small boy, perhaps three years old, riding a tricycle and zigzagging from side to side. His father, walking a few yards behind him, shouted, "Stop zigzagging. Go straight." The boy stopped riding, turned his head toward his father, looked at him quizzically, turned back around, and started zigzagging again. At this point the father caught up to the boy and shouted in a menacing tone, "I thought I told you to stop zigzagging. Do it again, and you're going to be in trouble." The boy quickly looked up and said, "Daddy, it's not me. It's the bike."

It is a humorous story, but there is also a message here. The situation is symbolic of what happens to children starting at birth and continuing throughout childhood. Both at home and at school, children are forever being admonished, corrected, and commanded: "What are you doing here?" "Stop doing that." "Put that away." "Come over here." "Don't talk like that." As a matter of self-defense, very early on, children learn to be defensive and to lie. This stays with them into adulthood, even after they have achieved success in life and hold important positions in business and government. Only then we call it "spinning."

INTERRUPTING/IGNORING/HALF-LISTENING

We treat children with disrespect when we don't listen to them, when we are easily distracted, when we don't give them our attention, when we ignore them. This occurs when a child says something, and we don't respond, or we change the subject without alluding to the child's remark; frequently, we interrupt to tell him to do something. Sometimes a friend or relative will ask a child a question, and before he can respond, the parent jumps in and answers for him. In each case, we are acting disrespectfully, and most of the time without the slightest notion that our behavior is inappropriate—although when our spouse, friend or parent does that to us, we become chagrined.

SUMMING UP

If we want children to grow up feeling respected and treating others with respect, we must interact with them in a courteous, considerate, and civil manner. We need to avoid sarcasm, belittling, yelling; we need to keep anger and impatience to a minimum; we need to avoid lying; we need to listen more and talk less; we need to command less and suggest and request more; we need to learn how to say "please," "thank you," "excuse me" "I'm sorry"—yes, even to children. This does not mean that as parents we must be saints—that we must never lose patience, act inappropriately, or never make demands. It does mean we will strive to be conscious of our mistakes, willing to admit them, be ready to make corrections, and that we will try to cultivate these values in our children. Most importantly, we will be role models for our children of respectful behavior when interacting with our spouses and others, young and old. And we will keep in mind that no child is too young to be treated with respect.

Need to Feel Important

Feeling important refers to a child's need to feel: "I have value. I am useful. I have power. I am somebody." This need is evident at a very early age. I recall observing a small child in an elevator, whose mother was about to press the button to select the floor. The child shouted, "No, no, me, me!" as she struggled on her tiptoes to press the button. Children want to do things for themselves, and so often we get in their way.

One morning I was having breakfast with a young mother and her small son in a highchair. The child was trying to feed himself and was getting food on his bib and his clothes. His mother grabbed his spoon and yelled, "Stop that. You're making a big mess. Here, I'll feed you." How nice it would have been if she had put her arm around him and said, "Isn't that great. You're trying to feed yourself."

On another occasion, a Junior High student told us that she came out second in a swim-meet, and her parents made her feel like a failure. It reminds me of our Olympic athletes who prepare, train, and sacrifice for many years and, if they don't win the gold medal, they feel like failures, even if they had won a silver medal. Imagine being second best in the world and feeling like a failure!

If children do not feel important (and this is a major problem for our young people today), if they don't develop a sense of value in constructive ways, they may seek negative ways to get attention. They may become rebellious, hostile, and antagonistic; they may engage in constant testing and struggling for power; they may join cliques or gangs, and they may turn to drugs, sex, crime, or violence. At the other extreme, they may become apathetic or withdrawn; they may lack initiative and ambition and become overly dependent on others.

One of the greatest challenges for parents, families, and communities is to find ways to help children develop this sense of importance. If we think about it, we will find innumerable ways to do this. The following are examples of how parents obstruct or enhance satisfaction of this need.

OVERPROTECTIVENESS

Parents diminish children's sense of power by limiting them too much. I, for one, was an overprotective parent. As a child growing up in New York City with both parents working, I had a lot of freedom. I ran the streets, and many times I felt lonely and frightened. Because of these feelings, when I became a father, I decided that my son was never going to feel the way I did. Guided by my fears, I became much too controlling. His mother also parented out of excess fear. It was not in our son's best interest and certainly not in ours. It created considerable and unnecessary discord and rebellion in our household.

Children need to experiment; they need to try things. That's the way they learn and grow, that's the way their sense of power grows. We need to encourage rather than inhibit their curiosity, their interest in experimentation, and their desire for adventure. We say "no" to children far too often. Children need many more "yes's" than "no's."

Certainly, we need to take measures to protect our children from real dangers, but we must also determine if we have imagined or exaggerated potential dangers. Fear often causes parents to confuse possibility with probability. Because something is possible, we frequently act as though it were probable. This is an important distinction for parents to keep in mind. By realizing that many things we fear are highly improbable, it can help us to say "yes" more often and to worry less. In the same vein, distinguishing between high- and low-risk activities can facilitate our decision-making process.

EXCESSIVE PERMISSIVENESS

The opposite of being overly protective is being too permissive. Yes, kids need more "yes's" than "no's" when they are growing up. However, if you never or rarely say "no" or try to satisfy all children's "wants," they might very well develop a false sense of entitlement and unrealistic expectations which will hurt them in the future as they come to grips with the realities of life. That is why it is important to distinguish between satisfying children's critical "needs" (which they deserve merely by existing) and satisfying their "wants" (which are subject to such criteria as age, maturity, and personalities of family members, family economics, and family values). Food and clothing are "needs" that must be satisfied, but eating junk food, scuba diving, or watching television all night represent "wants" which are another matter. However, even when saying "no" to any "want," it is important to do so in a way that honors the five critical needs. This may mean explaining the reasons for the rejection and listening and responding to the child's reactions.

TALKING TOO MUCH/NOT LISTENING

Parents often contribute to a child's sense of powerlessness by talking too much and not listening enough. We talk; we lecture; we give advice; we tell them how to feel and what to think; we overpower them with words when we should be listening and paying attention more to what they are saying, thinking, and feeling. Not listening says to the child, "I am not interested in what you have to say; you are not important enough for me to listen to." Listening says, "I care about what you have to say. You are important to me."

One of the most valuable assets in interpersonal relations—which too few people possess—is the ability to give someone you are with your undivided attention—the feeling of being the most important person in the world at that moment. It is especially important with children to listen attentively and to be fully present. This does not necessarily require lots of time. Even if you can only spare a few minutes, put other things aside and give the child your total attention—acting as though, for those few minutes, there is no one and nothing else more important.

When we listen to children, we not only give them a sense of importance, but we learn more about them. Further, they will want to listen more to us, creating many opportunities for us to influence them in positive, constructive ways.

DECISION MAKING

When parents are all knowing, all powerful—making all decisions and solving all problems—children miss an opportunity to grow in self-confidence. Involving children in decision-making and problem-solving, asking their opinions and listening to their answers, contributes to their sense of "I am somebody."

People do not, at a certain age, magically develop good judgment and become expert decision-makers. They become good at making bigger and better decisions by having experience at making smaller decisions along the way.

There are innumerable opportunities to involve children in decision-making at every age level. Whether it is about solving a family problem, preparing a menu for a family meal, planning a family activity, deciding what clothes to wear, or caring for a pet, children can be involved. Whenever possible, we need to ask our children's opinions, give them choices, and let them make their own decisions appropriate to their age and maturity, and we should be available to discuss their decisions with them. This is a way children can learn about their strengths and weaknesses and grow in their decision-making ability and confidence.

In addition to helping children feel important, you will be pleasantly surprised at what they have to say. One father, when discussing over dinner his desire to change jobs because he was unhappy with his present position, asked his teenage children what they thought. His daughter inquired why he was unhappy, and after he mentioned the reasons, she responded, "How do you know it will be any different somewhere else?" The ensuing discussion caused him to stop and think. He had not really taken his best shot at changing conditions where he was, or at looking at his own weaknesses, which contributed to his present unhappiness. His daughter's question made him realize that his problems could very well follow him to the next place.

SUMMING UP

Don't do everything for your children. Share tasks, household chores, responsibilities, authority, and accountability. From the earliest age, gradually provide them with more and more complex tasks to perform both for themselves and for the family.

Many areas of family life afford opportunities for children to participate and contribute in a meaningful way. Parents need to avoid being all powerful, solving all family problems, making all decisions, doing all the work, controlling everything that happens. Involve your children. Ask their opinions, give them things to do, share decision-making and power, give them status and recognition, and have patience with mistakes when it takes a little longer or is not done as well as you could have done yourself. Yes, children need to feel important. If we provide constructive, meaningful ways to make that happen, they will not need to engage in inappropriate, destructive activities to attempt to convince themselves and others that "I am somebody."

Need to Feel Accepted

Children have a need to feel accepted as individuals in their own right, with their own uniqueness, and not treated as mere reflections of their parents, as objects to be shaped in the image of what parents believe their ideal child should be like. This means that children have a right to their own feelings, opinions, ideas, concerns, wants, and needs. Too often we put down children because we don't like a feeling or opinion they express, or we ignore, trivialize, or ridicule their feelings and concerns. When we do so, it negatively affects communication and weakens the relationship. If we don't listen to their feelings, they may fester and surface later as inappropriate or destructive behavior. There is also less chance that children will express concerns or come to us for help with problems when it might be important for them to do so.

We need to recognize that feelings are not right or wrong; they just are. Acceptance does not imply liking or agreeing, nor does it have anything to do with condoning behavior. In fact, confusing feelings and desires with behavior is one of the problems parents have. Accepting a child's feelings is simply recognition that like all individuals, children have feelings too, and that a child's feelings are not to be suppressed or feared but rather to be understood and discussed.

OVERREACTING/EMOTIONALITY

At a workshop for teenagers, an 18-year-old high school senior related the following interaction with his parents: When asking for permission to join several friends for an overnight sleep-out on the Santa Monica beach following their senior prom, his father replied, "What, are you crazy? Don't you know how many muggings there are in Los Angeles?" His mother joined in, "It's out of the question!" According to the son, both parents abruptly walked out of the room without waiting for a response.

This emotional reaction on the part of the parents was obviously motivated by fear of their son engaging in what they perceived as a dangerous activity, something that any parent might easily identify with. But the son hadn't done anything. He was only asking for permission, expressing a desire. Their hasty, negative response—both the content and manner of delivery—was insensitive to their son's feelings. The rhetorical parental response, "What, are you crazy?" implies that there is something wrong with someone who would have such a desire.

A parent who accepts the child's right to his desires and is not overcome by fear and emotion, responds differently. For example, "Yes, I guess it would be exciting, but I have some reservations; with the kind of crimes that are occurring these days, it would make me very nervous. Let's think about it, and we'll discuss it some more." By accepting the child's desire, we can prevent bad feelings from developing. Because we are considerate of the child's feelings, we can discuss the situation with a greater probability of finding an amicable solution, either by easing the parents' fears or coming up with an alternative suggestion.

At a workshop for parents, a mother related that her child had received a bicycle for Christmas; a month later they were shopping at a mall when the child, noticing a better quality and fancier bike in a store window exclaimed, "Gee, would I like to have that one!" The mother retorted, "You ungrateful child! You just got a new bicycle for Christmas, so how can you be so greedy?" Yet the child was only expressing a desire.

Very often we overreact without thinking and hold children to a higher standard than we ourselves can meet. Haven't we, as adults, sometimes regretted a purchase after seeing something more desirable a few weeks later? Had the mother simply said, "Yes, I guess it would be nice to have the latest model, but do you know why you can't have it?" The child might have replied, "Sure, because I just got one." Whatever the child's response might have been, at least the parent would have been able to engage her in a parent-child conversation—something kids say they often do not have.

SUPPRESSING FEELINGS

We often do children a disservice by attempting to talk them out of their feelings. For example, a child is upset because a friend is mad at him and the parent says, "Don't be silly; he's not worth thinking about. Anyway, you have plenty of other friends." Now the child may feel twice as bad—first because the friend is still mad at him and then because the parent suggests he is silly for feeling bad. The parent may be well-intentioned, not wanting the child to be unhappy; sometimes the parent is frustrated, feeling that the child is too sensitive to what other kids think. Parents want to fix things,

make everything okay, protect the child from feeling hurt—
that's a parent's job, isn't it?

However, the message may not be comforting or enlightening. It may convey the idea that being upset when something
negative happens is bad. In addition to causing discomfort
for the child, it is a conversation stopper and denies the child
an opportunity to explore his feelings. A parent, who understands that feelings aren't right or wrong, and that the child
has a right to his own feelings, won't try to talk him out of
them. Acting in this light, a parent may respond simply by
saying: "I guess it hurts when a good friend is mad at you."
The parent might also identify with the child, recalling similar feelings when the parent was a child. Here the message is
that it's okay to have these feelings. The child's distress may
be of very short duration in any case, and it might have disap-
peared quickly, even had the parent said nothing.

Parents don't always have to do something about a child's
hurt feelings. Just being there and listening may be enough
to comfort the child. When a child's bad feelings persist
and are affecting the child negatively, the parent can help the
child explore those feelings and consider different alternatives for handling them. How much better than having a child
be ashamed of feelings, bury them, and have them come out
in negative ways, perhaps at unanticipated or inopportune
times.

BEING OVERLY CRITICAL

Another barrier to satisfying the need to feel accepted is
when parents criticize their children excessively. When this
happens, children may develop a low opinion of themselves,
tune out the criticism, or feel defeated, expressing an attitude
such as, "What's the use? I'll never satisfy them."

On the other hand, they may become frustrated and combat-
ive, causing parent-child interactions to become disagreeable

skirmishes. The reasons for the criticisms or negativity may be valid or invalid, reasonable or unreasonable, or a mixture of both, but too much can put a damper on conversation and negatively affect the relationship. Parents need to overlook many things. There is a saying in business that applies to parenting as well: "Don't sweat the small things." Parents don't have to react to everything. The establishment of regular family meetings will go a long way toward creating the atmosphere for much-needed, sustained parent-child dialogue.

POSITIVE REINFORCEMENT

We should be emphasizing the positive with children—looking for things to acknowledge. In a best-selling, management book, *The One Minute Manager,* by Kenneth Blanchard and Spencer Johnson, a major point is the need to catch people doing something right and to tell them about it. Unfortunately, we are very good at catching people doing something wrong, especially children. We need to change the emphasis to catching them doing something right. Children need more acknowledgments than put-downs. If we look for occasions to praise, we will find them, and as we praise more, such occasions will multiply. It should not be false praise but rather praise for a real accomplishment, something specific, not so general as to have little meaning. When having to criticize, focus on the behavior and not the person. When having to reject, do so with love and not with anger. For example, "I'm sure it would be exciting to spend the night on the beach with your friends, and I hate to disappoint you by saying no, but it would make me too nervous," rather than saying, "What, are you crazy?"

SUMMING UP

Accepting children means listening, trying to understand them, and accepting their right to their own points of view, feelings, desires, opinions, concerns, and ideas. If we act in a way that condemns or ridicules feelings or opinions of children, the implication may be that there is something wrong with them. When that happens, you reduce the chances of their listening to you and of your being able to influence them. Acceptance is not permissiveness. It's not giving children free license to act in any way they wish. Also, remember the distinction between *wants* and *needs*. You never will be able to satisfy all of your child's *wants*, nor would it be good for a child if you could. On the other hand, children acquire at birth the right to have their critical emotional needs satisfied, and as parents we must make every effort to do so. Accept your children as people in their own right and act accordingly. Recognize their accomplishments, don't sweat the small stuff, emphasize the positive, and when you must say "no," do so with love. Don't forget, your needs have to be satisfied too, if you are to become the best parent you can be. So relax, nourish yourself, and enjoy the journey.

Need to Feel Included

Children need to feel included. They need to feel they belong, to feel a part of things, to feel connected to other people, to have a sense of community. John Gardner, former Secretary of Health, Education and Welfare, once said that the problem with our cities is that they are not communities, but rather encampments of strangers. Sometimes it's that way with families.

So how do we create this sense of community, this connect-edness to others? That's why kids join cliques, gangs, clubs, and teams—to satisfy that need to belong. This happens when people engage with others in activities and projects, when they experience things together in a meaningful way. It is important for the family to create these opportunities.

People who do things together feel closer to one another. Family activities offer a way to become closer and also to have fun, learn, and contribute to others. Identifying strongly with the family unit makes children more resistant to outside, negative influences and more open to positive role models within the family. Obviously, children can't be included in everything, but we need to make a conscious effort to create family activities that appeal to all.

ACTIVITIES

Childhood is a time of curiosity and experimentation. Family activities can be used to have children try new things, broaden their interests, and strengthen their relations with other family members. Appendix B, *Family Activities List*—is a comprehensive list of over 150 different activity categories. Together family members can seek out activities *that everyone can participate in, enjoy, and learn from.*

There can be special activity evenings such as current events, jokes and humor, videos, movies, board games, cards, learning magic tricks, and much more. Sometimes a question and answer activity can be interesting and fun. For example, each person makes up a question or selects one from a book such as *The Kids Book of Questions* (see Appendix A— Stock, G.). The family then discusses the questions, one at a time. One question I like is, "You're walking down the street and you find a wallet with a $100 in it? What do you do? (a) go to the nearest police station and turn it in; (b) go home to your parents and ask them what to do; (c) take out the $100, throw the wallet away, find some friends, and have a good time." When a child selects (c), instead of preaching to him why that is bad, asking the reason for this response might be more valuable to learn something about how the child thinks. One response offered by a child to whom I asked the question was, "Well, if I took the money to the police station, it would never get back to the person who lost it. The policeman would probably keep it for himself—so better me than him." That could open up a discussion about police, honesty, and so on— perhaps even a visit to a police station.

When activities are repeated on a regular basis they can become traditions and rituals that can satisfy the need to feel included and secure. (See Chapter 4, *Game Plan #7*, for examples of this.)

PARENTS' WORKLIFE

Including children in your worklife has multiple benefits. Describe to them where you work, what you do, with whom you work, and how you feel about your work and your fellow workers. Include anything that will help them better understand that part of your life. If possible, take them to your workplace, introduce them to co-workers, and show them your office. Encourage them to ask questions and afterward, find out what they think about their visit—what impressed them, what they learned. If you work at home, or do freelance jobs, or have your own business, introduce them to clients and co-workers, and possibly have them do some work for you or with you. Since work is such an important part of your life, the children will feel more connected to you. They will learn a little more about who you are. When you and your spouse discuss something that happened at work, they will likely show more interest and be able to learn from the way you face situations and challenges. It would provide an opportunity for you to ask their opinion and get their reactions and learn about their thinking. An early introduction to what the work environment involves can be beneficial.

COMMUNICATION

"Communication is the lifeblood of an organization—the glue that holds everything together and the lubricant that keeps everything moving." This is a quotation I once read somewhere that sounds right for families, too. Unfortunately, communication is not an area of family strength. Parent-child communications too often are brief, fleeting, dull, or haphazard—more like interviews than conversations or discussions:

"Where are you going?" "Out."
"What are you going to do?" "Nothing."
"Who are you going with?" "Friends."
"Make sure you get back in time for dinner." "Okay."

Consequently, despite their best intentions, caring parents have little understanding about what kids are thinking or feeling. Meanwhile, children often feel misunderstood and puzzled by parent actions and frustrated by what they feel are attempts to control and overprotect them.

At a national TV forum, on the anniversary of the Columbine High School shooting, with teachers, parents, business people, community representatives, and high schools students participating, the problem came sharply into focus. The adults stressed the need for parents to supervise kids more closely; for example, knowing at all times what they are watching on TV, what they are doing, where they are, and whom they are with—including more rules and strict discipline for violations.

Another perspective on the problem was eloquently articulated by one of the high school students stating with fervor that the adults were "over the top" in thinking that they could watch and control kids 24 hours a day. The same student advised parents to learn to trust kids, to listen to them and be available when things went wrong, and to lighten up so that their kids could feel comfortable in confiding in them from time to time. The student finished his remarks by beseeching the adults to become better role models, not better preachers or policemen—especially if they ever expect to have any real influence on the kids.

To illustrate the gap that has to be bridged, here are a few typical examples of parent and children's written questionnaire responses at workshops.

Questionnaire Item: Briefly write down one question, concern, or problem you have regarding parent-child relations:

Typical Responses—High School Students

- They yell too much about things that are not relevant.

- How to convince parents when they think they are always right?

- They seem to have given up on me.

- Why are parents always so skeptical?

- How to be truthful when I don't feel they are truthful with me?

- Over-reaction makes me feel worse about school than I already feel.

- Not feeling comfortable in talking to them about problems and feelings.

Typical Responses—Parents

- How do I get my child to do his homework? He says it's boring.

- My child's room is like a pig's pen. What can I do about it?

- How to deal with stubborn behavior without resorting to screaming or spanking.

- I am concerned that my reactions to situations may be causing our children to turn away from us.

- Inability to get any response to open-ended questions regarding relationships.

- How can you effectively discipline without breaking the child's spirit/curiosity?

- My kids fight all the time. It drives me nuts.

- When you trust your child and find that she has been lying to you, what do you do to get back trust and respect?

Parents generally express frustration and concern at not being able to get their children to do what they expect and at not knowing what to do next. They seem unaware that children have emotional needs that are not being met. The net result is a vicious cycle where the lack of communication causes diminished trust, which in turn causes more guarded communication, leaving both parent and child frustrated. What exacerbates the situation is the lack of any meaningful discussion between parent and child about the issues. This is why family inadequacies are passed on from one generation to the next.

The challenge for parents is to move from sporadic, brief interchanges to sustained and substantive dialogue. Family meetings and especially feedback sessions provide settings and context for this to happen.

FAMILY AS A COMMUNITY

I like the concept of the family as a community—a community whose well-being is dependent on the quality of its decisions, cooperation of its members, sense of belonging, and positive feelings of regard for one another. An explicit goal is to interact with one another in ways that satisfy the five critical needs of each person—and where all members share in the tasks and responsibilities of the family. The concept of the family as a learning community is an important one. It is a concept that should be expressed and demonstrated early and discussed often with the children.

Family Meetings

Family meetings can be a major activity for parents and children to assess how well they are doing, individually and collectively, and to decide on ways to make things better. Thus, a sense of community is created through sharing feelings, information, and experiences. Participation in these types of meetings contributes knowledge and skills that will be invaluable to children throughout their lives.

Goal Oriented Meetings (periodic, as needed)

The family attempts to achieve consensus in regard to assigning family responsibilities/tasks, establishing family rules, problem solving, decision making, and project planning.

I was impressed with one family's approach to household chores. Instead of the traditional practice of parents delegating tasks to their kids and following up with non-stop nagging, they held a family meeting to decide on responsibilities together. First a list was compiled of all the things that had to be done for the family to function. They then checked off the things that only the parents were capable of doing. (The kids were impressed; they hadn't realized how many things their parents were doing.) All remaining tasks were then discussed, and a consensus reached on who was going to be responsible for each one.

One child was in charge of caring for the family dog. Not only did she get this job, but she got a title too, "Director of Animal Husbandry." She was also asked to prepare and administer a budget. Once the others approved the budget, the daughter received the money and full control. Another child became Safety Director. Among other things, he was responsible for identifying potential safety hazards and alerting the family to them. He was doing a good job until he decided to have a fire drill at 1 a.m. (That almost cost him his job!) Finally, everyone received one or more jobs and titles, with the opportunity to contribute to the family and acquire new skills. At periodic follow-up meetings, family members report on progress, discuss problems and solutions, and exchange feedback.

Family Feedback Meetings
(ongoing, 1 x weekly or 2 x monthly)

Parents set aside time to address all concerns, feelings, and problems in an open, supportive climate—where the family as a whole asks, "How are we doing as a family and as individuals, and what could we be doing differently and better?" The one agenda item is: "What do we see one another, or ourselves, doing that is hindering or helping us to lead happy, healthy, productive lives?" Individuals have an opportunity to give and receive feedback, and to talk about what's going on in their lives, and ask for or offer help.

Some families have started regular family feedback sessions. In one such session, Sally, a divorced working mother, met with her three children, Pamela 12, Robert 11, and Tony 7. She started the meeting by sharing her guilt feelings about not spending enough time with her kids. Robert responded by agreeing that she was neglecting them. Pamela felt that Robert should stop complaining and help his mother more. Tony was quiet. Sally reviewed her outside activities with them—her job, church, and occasional social activities—remarking that they didn't seem overwhelming. Robert reminded her that she had left out one important category. When Sally asked him to be specific, he responded by saying, "Miscellaneous, you are being 'miscellaneoused' to death." Further discussion supported Robert. Sally was constantly being asked to participate on various work, church, political, and civic committees and had a hard time saying "no." As a result of this meeting, she reconsidered her priorities and made some changes in her lifestyle.

In one elementary school, where 2nd grade class feedback meetings were held weekly, one teacher asked the children what she had done that week that they liked or didn't like. One of the kids said that he was upset when a girl in his class cried.

"Why were you upset?" the teacher inquired.

"Well, I don't like when people cry—only girls and sissies cry, and you should have stopped her."

"Do any of you other boys or girls ever feel like crying?" the teacher asked.

"I feel like crying sometimes when my parents get angry with me," a boy replied.

"And do you cry then?" asked the teacher.

"Oh, no," replied the boy, "only girls and sissies cry."

At which point, one little boy in the back of the room raised his hand and said, "Teacher, I think girls cry on the outside, and boys cry on the inside."

These sessions can create an atmosphere where children are more willing to share their fears, concerns, and questions about school, health, sex, and other subjects, which they typically might be embarrassed or reticent to discuss with parents—also, where parents might be more willing to share their own feelings and family problems. In this way, these sessions contribute to children feeling included as an integral part of the family, and they also learn to appreciate their parents more as people—not just as mom and dad.

SUMMING UP

Children need to feel included and connected. Problems in schools and families in recent years have caused us to realize that there are more troubled children than just the ones who commit violence, attempt suicide, and use drugs, and this includes the academically successful also. If parents are to be positive influences on children, a strong sense of community must be developed. This can be accomplished by doing things together and providing children with opportunities to take an active part in family affairs.

Select activities that all family members will find interesting and worthwhile. Have children participate in the selection. Make a conscious decision to include them in as many choices, discussions, and decisions as possible as part of their everyday lives. Have children participate in meetings held periodically—as appropriate to their age, maturity, and the family situation. These meetings can contribute to skill development in communication, decision-making, problem solving, and other life skills.

To stay healthy and happy, families need to know how well they are doing—what their weaknesses, concerns, and problems are, and what they can do about them; also, how they can capitalize and make best use of their strengths and assets, and how they can use one another as helping resources. A weekly family feedback session and other family meetings are recommended to serve this purpose and contribute to the quality of life of the individuals and the family as a whole.

Need to Feel Secure

Children need to feel secure. Security means creating a positive environment where people care about one another and show it; where people express themselves and others listen; where differences are accepted and conflicts are resolved constructively; where enough structure and rules exist for children to feel safe and protected, and where children have opportunities to actively participate in their own evolution and that of the family.

The following is a discussion of important elements contributing to a child's sense of security.

RELATIONSHIP OF PARENTS

Parents are primary role models for children. When parents bicker, treat each other disrespectfully, and rarely show affection, children experience anxiety and insecurity. As one young student said, "I used to see my parents argue and fight. That wouldn't have been so bad, except I never saw them make up." Some children have felt that they were somehow the cause of their parents not getting along. During a discussion at the end of a seminar, one parent remarked, "Wow, what a revelation—my husband and I have these same five needs." The group consensus was that if couples treated each other with these five needs in mind, they would be better role models for the kids, and there would be happier marriages, fewer divorces, and more secure, joyful children.

A CARING, AFFECTIONATE ENVIRONMENT

Among other things, a caring environment is one in which family members show affection toward one another. Observing affection between parents and receiving affection from them is very important to the child's sense of security.

Beginnings and endings are especially important. How you begin and end the day, week, month, and year presents opportunities for regular demonstrations of affection. Parents often tell me that their days begin chaotically. They go to the kids' room and yell, "Okay, get out of bed, you are going to be late for school. If I have to tell you one more time, then no dessert or allowance this week." One parent told us, "My mother didn't do that. She would come to my room, stroke my hair softly, and quietly say, 'Honey, it's time to get up; get ready for school sweetheart.' Then she yelled at me." At least this mother was headed in the right direction.

At another workshop, a mother related how she got fed up with having to yell, threaten, and fight with her kids to get them out of bed in the morning. She finally decided to put an end to it. She met with them one evening and announced that (1) she would no longer wake them—that was their responsibility; (2) they all had to be at breakfast at a specific time; and (3) if they failed to comply, they would have to prepare breakfast themselves, and she would not drive them to school. And she did this without expressing anger. The other parents in the group held their collective breaths and asked, "What happened?" She responded, "For two days, the kids made their own breakfast and missed school. On the third day, they were on time, and I drove them to school, and it continues that way to this day." It took her a long time to get to that point, but she finally realized a caring environment also meant caring about herself.

TRADITION AND RITUALS

Establishing traditions and rituals to celebrate events give children a sense of stability and security. In addition to the usual holiday and birthday celebrations and vacations, one could schedule a weekly or monthly dinner at which family members share something for which they feel particularly thankful; another could be a discussion dinner where some special topic is explored (e.g., current events, human interest, sports); a special story evening where each person shares a story and leads a discussion; any of the various family meetings could become traditions; trips to explore the city could be fun and have value; and volunteering service to a charity or a charitable event could become an important annual experience. Especially worthwhile would be a family activity that has health benefits such as cycling, jogging, walking, or swimming together.

PARENT ANXIETY

Parents never stop worrying about their kids, no matter how old they are, and rarely stop treating them as children, even after they become adults. My mother was a world-class worrier. One of my favorite stories is about arriving at a hotel in Denver and receiving a call from her. She called to admonish me to go to bed early because I had a cold when I left Los Angeles. My brother, who was with me on a lecture tour, picked up the phone, and responded, "Mom, the kid is 54 years old, he can decide when to go to bed."

Worry is a natural phenomenon for parents, but with some families it is so pronounced that children grow up in an atmosphere of fear and trepidation, where the pervasive feeling is that danger is everywhere, and the next tragedy is just around the corner. Overprotective, excessively controlling parents often produce insecure, uptight, anxious kids who carry some of these hang-ups and anxieties into adulthood. These parents create a burden for themselves and their children. One of the most significant things parents can do for a child is to create an environment where the adults are relaxed, happy, interested in life, and enjoying it. This is why it is so important for parents to nurture themselves and make this a priority in their lives.

DISCIPLINE

What about discipline? Discipline is important as one factor that could contribute positively to a child's sense of security, if clearly understood and properly administered. Unfortunately, that has often not been the case. In practice, it has meant punishing a child for misbehaving, with the punishment and what constituted unacceptable behavior changing, depending on the mood or whimsy of the parents. And to make matters worse, each parent might have a different view of a given situation. This inconsistency and ambiguity creates confusion and insecurity for parents and children and causes conflict, but it doesn't have to be that way.

All communities need limits, rules, and consequences, and so do families. Children need structure, without which they will not feel secure. Their own impulses and inexperience can put them in danger. Parents, too, need structure to provide stability for the family in order to cope with their multiple responsibilities and the fast pace of a changing society. Here is where the concept of the family as a learning community once more becomes relevant.

The process of establishing rules and consequences together in family meetings is a workable approach that makes sense and has multiple side benefits. It gives everyone an investment in making it work and increases the probability that it will. Most important, it is an opportunity to make a strong contribution to satisfying the five critical emotional needs of children. Besides being a wonderful civics lesson, it will contribute to bringing the family closer together and has possibilities of enhancing the children's skills in critical thinking, writing, reading, discussion, negotiation, and compromise.

For every rule there should be a reason. If you can't think of a reason, why have the rule in the first place? In general, rules and consequences should apply to everyone—parents included. If not, children will lose respect for the process and will feel justified in circumventing rules. Some rules may be children-specific and others parent-specific because they are not applicable to everyone.

Consequences are necessary for anyone who breaks a rule. Rather than punish, the purpose of consequences should be to remind us why we have the rule in the first place. And wherever possible, a consequence should be related to the infraction. For example, one parent, upon discovering that her son had stolen a toy from a store, simply said that, "In our family, we don't take things from one another without permission, nor do we steal things from others." To the child's considerable chagrin, she then accompanied the boy to the store to return the toy and apologize. The manager accepted the apology, and explained that if it happened again, he would have to call the police.

In establishing rules and consequences, consensus should be sought. The benefits of achieving consensus are such that the effort should not be given up easily. Whenever a consensus cannot be achieved, and a decision needs to be made, the parents are always the final authority, and children need to understand this from the outset. Some rules will be non-negotiable. This is another opportunity for kids to experience how the "real world" works. When this becomes necessary, non-negotiable doesn't mean no discussion. Parents are encouraged to take time to explain the reasons and to listen to children's comments.

It is important to start this process early in the life cycle of the family, and continue with ongoing review, evaluation, and revisions. An annual meeting to evaluate the past year and to consider proposals for change could become a tradition. Children would participate fully to the degree that their age and maturity permit.

When I present the above concepts in lectures and workshops, some parents react negatively, even though what they are doing is not working. Some fear they would be giving up authority and would lose control. Others state that a family is not a democracy and shouldn't be. I find it interesting that we see no contradiction in preparing children to participate in a democratic society by raising them in autocratic homes and schools. Perhaps this is one of the reasons why the "vote"— one of the most precious rights we have in our democracy—is exercised by such a low percentage of eligible voters, young and old of both major parties.

Further Thoughts on Discipline

In seeking consensus and guiding the family toward shared responsibility and accountability, it is important for parents to emphasize the need for reasonable limits and consequences. Also, rules should not be carved in stone. Keep an experimental attitude; add, delete, and revise rules as you learn more about what's fair, reasonable, and workable. The elements described below are considered pitfalls to avoid.

Ambiguous Expectations

Rules and consequences regarding key areas of living— e.g., personal hygiene, responsibilities, meals, sleep, health, recreation, meetings, personal rights, TV, computer, homework, fighting—need to be stated with enough specificity so that everyone understands the same thing, including why each one is important and that the agreed upon consequences are appropriate.

Too Many Rules

Start with a few basic rules that are necessary for daily living where problems already exist, or can be anticipated;

otherwise add rules as circumstances arise. Don't become overwhelmed with a large number of rules at the outset.

Excessive Limits

Setting arbitrary, inflexible limits frequently results in non-compliance and tension, leaving both parent and child as adversaries. Once you appear to have a consensus, test for agreement to make sure individuals are not just acquiescing, but are definitely in accord.

Inappropriate/Excessive Consequences

Such punishment is usually difficult to enforce, is frequently viewed as unjust, and consequently provides little learning, as the violator may be preoccupied with the unfairness of the situation, even though consensus was thought to have been achieved. Once again, test for agreement before the final decision.

Inconsistent Implementation of Consequences

When consequences are not implemented consistently or taken lightly, the process loses credibility, and the rules will have less and less meaning. A warning in place of a consequence should be avoided unless it becomes part of the process. Exceptions can be made as long as there is a consensus, and they are not mistaken for a precedent.

Physical Punishment

Physical punishment needs to be avoided. It deals with symptoms and often delays or even prevents solutions. Sometimes the wrong lessons are learned, and there may be unintended consequences. When we hit a child, the lesson might be that it's all right to use force if you are bigger and stronger. Reactions to force are frequently delayed, but strong. A child who is paddled by a principal can't do anything immediately, but he might come back on the weekend to vandalize the school. After being spanked by a parent, a child may take it out on a younger sibling or schoolmate.

Self-Discipline

Self-discipline needs to be encouraged and developed. This means allowing children to explore more things and experience the consequences of their actions. In this way, they learn to anticipate negative consequences and exercise self-control to avoid them. Too much control deprives children of this opportunity.

SUMMING UP

Children need freedom as much as control; to smother them can result in intimidated children or rebellious ones. One goal is to protect them so they don't suffer from their impulses and inexperience; another is for them to have enough freedom to grow into confident, self-reliant, thoughtful, independent, caring, civic-minded individuals. Growing up in a positive environment contributes to a child's sense of security. Seeing parents in a loving, respectful relationship is of utmost importance. Traditions and rituals add to a sense of stability and security.

Discipline is a much discussed and controversial subject. It should not be viewed as an entity in itself, but rather as a component of security. Parents are the recognized family leaders and, as such, will always be the final authority. Ideally, they will relate to their children and influence them from a position of moral leadership, and not just power. This calls for increasing opportunities for children to self-govern and participate in contributing to and managing the conditions of their existence. Having children be an integral part of the process will increase the probability of creating rules and consequences that are appropriate and consistent. Furthermore, they are more likely to be understood and supported. Consequently, the need for discipline will decline, and self-discipline is more likely to develop. In addition, the process can be an excellent learning experience for children (and parents, too), to enhance skills in reading, writing, listening, speaking, decision-making, negotiation, compromise, and community participation.

What About Love?

Perhaps you have asked yourself, "What about love? Why hasn't love been included as one of the five critical needs of children?" It was omitted purposefully, not because it lacks importance—on the contrary, it is extremely important—but rather because the word "love" has lost some of its force and meaning through overuse and misuse.

In many cases, saying the words "I love you" has become trite, meaningless, or confusing. In a scene from the movie *Nuts,* a conversation takes place between a mother and her estranged daughter: The mother says to the daughter, "You know we love you sweetheart, don't you? Didn't we always tell you we loved you?" To which the daughter replies angrily, "Love? What do you know about love? You told me you loved me, but you never showed me you did." Yes, there is a difference.

There are parents who abuse or neglect their children and then say, "I love you," thinking it makes up for their behavior. Too often, love is equated with saying "I love you." If saying "I love you" were enough, we might not have such a high divorce rate. Marriages don't break up because a spouse stops saying "I love you." They break up because spouses quit treating each other in a loving way.

Most parents love their children or so we assume. However, we cannot assume from this that most parents act in a loving way. My answer to "What about love?" is that loving your child is essential and saying "I love you" is important, but neither is sufficient unless you act in a loving way. That is why I define "acting in a loving way" as relating to children in ways that make the child feel *respected, important, accepted, included,* and *secure*—that's the best way to say, "I love you."

Concluding Thoughts

Understanding the five critical needs of children provides the basis for parenting that is forward-looking and action-oriented. This approach applies to children of all age groups and segments of society. It provides parents with a concrete framework to guide their interactions with children, and gives them a practical tool for evaluating how things are going. Further, parents tell us that they have the same five needs as their kids and that if they focused on these needs, their relationship would be stronger, they would be better role models for the kids, and it would add substantially to their children's sense of security, and to the stability and well-being of the family.

The concept of the five critical needs calls for parents to focus on emotional health, not only the child's, but their own. They must nurture themselves in order to be good role models for their children. Above all, enjoy your children; have fun with them and the experience of parenting. When your behavior is "off" in some way—you lose your cool, you make a mistake, you do something you wish you hadn't—don't be too hard on yourself. Don't expect to be perfect. Relax! It's part of being human. Remember, having happy, relaxed parents is a great gift we can give our children.

The concept of the five needs of children makes the parenting task easier. Children have these five needs throughout their lives. So, although children at different ages and stages of development may act differently, have different problems, and express their personalities in particular ways, these five needs remain constant. This enables parents to apply the principles of the five needs under all circumstances and in all situations. It gives parents continuous practice in relating to children in emotionally healthy ways. It provides a focus and guidelines for their everyday interactions with children and helps them parent with confidence and consistency. And when children sense that parents know what they are doing, it adds to the youngsters' sense of security.

TWO

Family Situations

*(A Closer Look at
Behavior That Helps
and Behavior That Hurts)*

Family Situations

In interacting with children, *how* you do something is as
important as *what* you do. Even the way we change an in-
fant's diaper communicates much to the child about our level
of caring and involvement. Offering children greater responsibility can make them feel important, but micro managing
the process and not giving any autonomy of action can make
them feel unimportant and limit their learning possibilities. If
a clear approach to child rearing is lacking, parent behavior is
likely to be inconsistent. Actions and reactions between parents and children in different family situations frequently are
based more on emotions than on reason.

In Chapter 1, many examples were presented on how inconsistent, reactive behavior interfered with satisfying the
emotional needs of children and parents. In this chapter, we
will take a more detailed look at how this plays out in everyday life. Described below are actual situations gathered from
conversations, interviews, seminars, and personal experiences. In each case, there is a discussion of what happened,
how it might have been handled more effectively, and its relation to the five critical needs of children.

45

SITUATION 1: RESPECT, ACCEPTANCE
(To Buy or Not To Buy?)

A 10th grader, while shopping with her father in a book-store, discovered a large, costly book of Shakespeare's works and asked, "Dad, would you please buy this book for me?"

Dad, obviously annoyed, replied: "Are you kidding? That's just what you need, a big expensive book like that! With all the time you spend watching television, you'd probably never open it."

The child, looking hurt, replied meekly: "But I'm doing well in school."

Behavior That Hurts

Rejecting the child's request in derogatory terms implies something is the matter with her for expressing this desire. The child is showing interest in something educationally de-sirable. Even if it's just an impulse or a whim, dismissing it out-of-hand cuts off communication. Dad's reaction is hurt-ful and provides little, if any, learning for his daughter.

Behavior That Helps

The following are suggested respectful and constructive alternative responses:

"It looks like a great book, and Shakespeare is a wonderful writer, but it's expensive. Let's get one or two of his plays from the library, and after you have read them, we'll buy something and start your own library. How does that sound?"

"How about if we get one of his plays and a biography from the library? We'll both read and discuss them and go from there. Ask your teacher to recommend which plays to read first."

Remarks

- ◆ Every interaction represents an opportunity to connect or disconnect with one's child.

- ◆ Here was a missed opportunity to try to connect with the child concerning education, money, and decision-making.

- ◆ We sometimes treat a child's expressed desire as though it were negative behavior.

- ◆ Accept a child's right to have unrealistic desires, even if you won't satisfy them.

- ◆ In rejecting a child's request, do so constructively, with respect.

- ◆ Negativity and sarcasm send the wrong message.

SITUATION 2: ACCEPTANCE, RESPECT
(Music Lover's Taste)

A teenage girl describes a conflict with her father as follows:

"Growing up in the sixties, my parents hated my music. I was constantly told to turn it down or turn it off. My father went so far as to institute a rule—for every hour of rock I listened to, I had to listen to one hour of classical music. It made me negative toward classical music."

Behavior That Hurts

The parents' hatred for the music, and objections to her listening to it, creates an adversarial relationship. Requiring her to listen to classical music does not create interest, but rather the opposite.

Behavior That Helps

To maintain positive relations, the father could express his own feelings about her music, but do so respectfully—his "holier than thou" attitude won't help. Regarding classical music, it would be more desirable and effective if the father would show his own interest and passion—let his daughter see the enthusiasm and positive feelings it evokes in him. Hopefully, her interest and curiosity would grow.

The father could invite her to listen with him to some recordings or attend a concert together. He could suggest a trade-off—he attends one of her events and she reciprocates.

Based on personal research or reading, he could also initiate a discussion with his daughter about the relationship between classical and rock music—this could be enlightening to both.

Remarks

♦ Here was an opportunity for the parent to connect with the child concerning music.

♦ Connecting is not possible if one party is inflexible, self-righteous, or disrespectful toward another's taste.

♦ Keeping an open mind can lead to mutual learning or, at least, to mutual tolerance.

♦ Accepting the daughter's right to her own taste in music increases the possibility of influencing her to expand her horizons.

♦ Selecting creative ways to stimulate another's interest is usually more productive than force-feeding.

SITUATION 3: INCLUSION, RESPECT, SECURITY
(Parental Secrecy)

A 12-year-old boy describes his feelings of rejection as follows:

> "One night I heard my mother and father in a loud argument in the other room. The next morning when I asked my mother what she and my father were arguing about, she replied, 'What goes on between me and your father is none of your business.' My feelings got smashed."

Behavior That Hurts

The mother's harshness in protecting her privacy is both unnecessary and harmful. The child's curiosity is crushed without the parent learning anything about the child's concerns. The mother's reaction might be displaced anger left over from the argument with her husband; it also might be the result of guilt or fear that her son might find out about a sensitive marital problem.

Behavior That Helps

The parent could have politely suggested that it was nothing her son needed to be concerned about, or that it was something she did not feel comfortable discussing at this time. She could have asked him why he was inquiring and then responded in a courteous and reassuring way. She might have decided to share some part of the argument of the night before in a limited or general way.

Remarks

♦ As parents, we can profit by examining our fears, anxieties, and taboos that tend to restrict effectiveness with our children. Such a review might help us expand areas of inclusion for our children and handle areas of privacy more effectively.

◆ Parents have a right to privacy but, when expressed with disdain, it can have negative effects.

◆ Parents need to accept a child's right to be curious or concerned about what's going on with parents.

◆ Sharing more with children, including concerns and problems, can reduce a child's anxieties and enhance feelings of belonging and security.

◆ Listening to and sharing with children increase the probability that they will do the same with you.

SITUATION 4: RESPECT, IMPORTANCE
(My Room, My Castle)

A young adult describes one way his parents made him feel important as he was growing up:

"My mother and father said my room was my own, and that's the way they treated it. They asked permission to enter, and would never go through my things without first asking. I was in charge of how to decorate it—it changed as I did. I felt that it was truly my world and, because it was respected, so was I."

Behavior That Hurts

The situation described above customarily is not the norm. In many cases, parents spend their children's teen years, and preteens too, nagging children about keeping their rooms clean—usually unsuccessfully. Typically, parents have not spelled out their expectations and the consequences for not meeting them. Even where they have been specified, these standards often change from week to week or moment to moment, with consequences deteriorating into idle threats. When consistent follow-through is lacking, the situation remains unresolved—the children annoyed by the constant harping, and the parents frustrated by the lack of compliance.

Behavior That Helps

In the above situation, the parents apparently recognized the value in respecting their son's privacy and in giving him responsibility for making decisions about his living environment. They showed confidence in his ability to handle this responsibility and evidently realized that he would benefit. It obviously contributed to his feelings of self-respect and importance.

Remarks

- Giving children increasing degrees of responsibility, until or unless they prove themselves incapable of handling it, will help them become more responsible.

- Too much control can limit the opportunity for development of a child's self-control.

- Letting go of control is difficult for most parents. It means learning to live with anxiety and managing it.

- Parents should assess risk and introduce safeguards accordingly. This includes inspecting a child's room when necessary.

- Parents should make a conscious effort to provide opportunities for children to grow in self-confidence.

SITUATION 5: Respect, Security
(Grandma and Grandpa
Know Best or Do They?)

One Saturday morning, Helen and her 8-year-old son Roger, are visiting Marsha and George, Helen's mother and father-in-law. Roger is sitting on the floor leafing through a magazine when Marsha suddenly yells at her grandson in an impatient, angry tone: "Roger, put the magazine down and clear away your toys this minute!" Roger says nothing and continues to look at the magazine.

The grandmother gets up, walks over to Roger, rips the magazine out of his hand, pulls him by the collar over to the toys, and says, "Now put these away, right now! When I tell you to do something, do it immediately."

She then turns to her daughter, Helen, and says, "Why don't you say something to him? Aren't you ever going to teach this kid some discipline? How can you allow him to be so disrespectful?"

Helen replies, "Mom, I don't think you should have yelled at him the way you did. Why didn't you just ask him in a nice way to pick up the toys?"

"Just wait, in a few years he'll be a teenager. Try to discipline him then, and he'll probably beat the hell out of you," shouts the grandfather angrily from across the living room.

According to Helen, Roger is generally a well-behaved child.

Behavior That Hurts

What is the grandmother's goal in this situation? Is it to teach Roger good habits, discipline, or respect for elders? Expecting instantaneous and automatic compliance from Roger to her jarring demand is unrealistic and ineffective.

Yelling and using physical force to impose her will seems exaggerated and counter-productive. Marsha's and George's hostility toward their daughter-in-law in front of her son poisons the atmosphere and creates an adversarial relationship. Roger can only be negatively affected by his grandmother's actions—either feeling guilty for having caused the situation or angry toward his grandparents because of the way they treated him and his mother.

Behavior That Helps

If the goal is to get the toys put away and for Roger to learn to take responsibility for doing so without being asked, the following are suggested approaches.

"Roger, would you do me a favor and put your magazine down for a minute, and put your toys away? I'm afraid someone might trip over them."

"Roger, it would help me if you put things away when you are through with them. Then I wouldn't have to do it. I'd appreciate it."

Remarks

- To promote courteous, respectful behavior in children, treat them respectfully.

- Children want to please their parents. A consistent, respectful, positive approach will reinforce that desire.

- When adult family members argue in front of their kids and treat one another disrespectfully, the children's sense of security is threatened.

SITUATION 6: SECURITY, INCLUSION, ACCEPTANCE
(Parents' Divorce)

A 16-year old describes his feelings regarding his parents' divorce as follows:

"As my father and mother's relationship deteriorated to the point of ending their 17-year-old marriage, I felt total rejection. When my father moved out of the house, I was devastated. It was at that time I started to experiment with drugs. I felt an incredible amount of anger and pain that we couldn't stay together like other families—that my father was going to start his life over, while leaving ours all screwed up."

Behavior That Hurts

Frequently parents do not realize that children may feel personally rejected, even somehow to blame, when a divorce occurs; they may underestimate the negative effects of divorce on children. Parents' expression of anger toward each other adds to children's trauma. Discussions with the children are often avoided because of feelings of fear, guilt, inadequacy, and confusion.

Behavior That Helps

Ideally, a plan should be worked out and implemented jointly by both parents which might include some of the following:

1. Joint and individual discussions with the children to reassure them of your love and their lack of blame for the divorce.

2. To reduce fear of the unknown, provide children with details about those things that will change and how it will affect them.

3. Try not to overwhelm children with too much at one time. A family meeting with a counselor could be very helpful.

Remarks

◆ The negative effects on a child's sense of security caused by divorce can be long-lasting and powerful.

◆ Parents can reduce adverse effects of divorce on children by including them in discussions before, during, and after the process—also by setting aside animosities for the good of the children.

◆ Parents should not be surprised at a child's anger or resistance to discussions. Accept anger and continue to do your best at listening, understanding, and reassuring.

SITUATION 7: ACCEPTANCE, INCLUSION, IMPORTANCE (Changing Baby's Diaper)

Anne had put her four-month-old Sarah on a table and abruptly started to change her diapers, with much resistance from the baby and lots of crying. The mother became increasingly more nervous and impatient with the baby. In a frustrated tone, the mother said such things as, "Now you stay still! You're going to get these diapers changed whether you like it or not." The child became increasingly upset as the mother's frustration increased.

The child's grandfather observed the interaction but didn't say anything until he got back to his home and telephoned his daughter. He tactfully suggested that his daughter might have reacted too impatiently and abruptly, that talking to the baby gently, and not just handling her, might have helped.

The next day the young mother called her father and told him that his advice had "made her day." She related that when the baby needed a change of diapers, she played with her first, then showed her two diapers, playfully encouraging her to make a choice, and proceeded to change her with no crying or fuss.

Behavior That Hurts

The baby's crying may have been a response to the abruptness of the change from play to diapers; this might have been especially true if the diaper change impetus came from a smell and not the baby's crying. The mother's nervousness and tone of voice exacerbated the discomfort already felt by the child from the bowel movement, and thus triggered the child's reaction. Being a first baby, the mother's inexperience was no doubt a factor.

Behavior That Helps

A four-month-old doesn't have words or vocabulary to express desires and frustrations. She relies on facial expressions, body movements, and sounds to convey her state of mind. A parent must be a patient, careful learner, listening and observing what the baby wants. A patient, playful attitude on the part of the parent is invaluable in having a calming and positive effect on the child.

Remarks

◆ Babies are not objects; they have feelings about how we treat them.

- Although babies can't speak, they do communicate. Parents need to be sensitive, aware listeners.

- The goal should not only be to get the task done, but also to have a positive, playful interaction with the child.

- Parents are not always fortunate enough to have someone observe the way they care for their child and who can provide constructive feedback. It is important for parents to become observers of their own behavior and to seek feedback from others.

- Involving children in choices can contribute to their sense of importance and security, even at the earliest ages, and though they may not fully comprehend the alternatives. In this way, parents start practicing the art of inclusion early on.

SITUATION 8: ACCEPTANCE, SECURITY
(To Let the Bird Fly or Not)

A happily married woman describes a tough choice that she and her parents made when she was 17 years old:

"After some in-depth discussions, my parents gave me a choice to live at home or to move out and live with my older boyfriend. My parents and I had been in constant conflict about my staying overnight at his apartment several times a week and breaking other rules. They stated in very strong terms their preference for me to stay at home under the conditions, which they spelled out, and said it would be very hard for them if I moved out. They stressed being tired of conflict, and if I stayed I would have to follow the rules. Once I made the decision, they allowed me to move out without recriminations."

Behavior That Hurts

Insisting that their daughter remain at home under the parent-imposed conditions was not working. Had the parents continued to insist, it probably would have led to further deterioration in their relations, with the daughter perhaps running away from home, and ending in a ruptured relationship.

Behavior That Helps

The parents put their fears and emotions aside in allowing their daughter to choose; they controlled their anxiety. The daughter spending evenings at the boyfriend's apartment resulted in ever-increasing tension, conflict, and unhappiness at home. The parents decided that the status quo was unhealthy for the entire family, which included two other siblings. They made sure the door was left open for the daughter to come back if the new situation did not work out.

Remarks

- Sometimes it's necessary to make the best out of a bad situation and choose between two alternatives, neither of which seems desirable.

- Giving a child responsibility for her own life, when it appears as a parent you cannot make the child do what you feel is right, is sometimes the best decision.

- Often the risks involved in a child's choice are not as dire as a parent imagines and can be reversed if things don't work.

- Accepting a decision with which the parent disagrees can enable the parent to maintain some influence in the long run.

◆ Including the child in decision-making enhances her sense of importance.

SITUATION 9: ACCEPTANCE, RESPECT, SECURITY (Forced Piano Playing)

How a father made a nine-year-old feel diminished is described as follows:

"I remember when my father made me feel like two cents because I didn't want to play the piano for guests at a Thanksgiving dinner at our house. He didn't ask me to play, he ordered me to. When I told him I didn't feel like it, he answered, 'What does that have to do with anything? Do you think I have the luxury of only doing things I feel like doing?' We got into an argument, with him calling me lazy and stubborn, which embarrassed me in front of the family."

Behavior That Hurts

The father fails to accept the child as an individual with feelings and needs of his own. He seems to look at his son's performance as a payoff for the money spent on lessons— "after all I've done for you" attitude. Parents often succumb to a common need to show off their children to others. The child's resistance becomes a challenge to parental authority and evokes their anger and disrespectful behavior toward the child.

Behavior That Helps

Parents need to think of how they would feel if someone in authority ordered them to perform; they need to recognize that children are not machines which can be turned on and off at will. Polite encouragement, with an escape clause, would be more appropriate and effective: "Carl, I'd love to have you play something for us, if you feel like it," or "Would you like to play something for us? I'm sure everyone would like to hear you."

Remarks

- A child's security is threatened if expected to perform under any circumstances, on command, and without consent.

- There are many situations like this where adults may succeed in forcing children to do something, but the amount of resentment and other unintended consequences can be costly.

- Parents need to get their egos out of the way and accept a child's right to say "no" in areas that should be consensual.

- Children are people too and can't be expected to always do what parents want them to do, on command.

- Approaching children with courtesy and respect, ordering less, and requesting more will pay off.

SITUATION 10: SECURITY, INCLUSION, IMPORTANCE
(Siblings Fighting/Parents' Despair)

Mary reports that her sons seem to be arguing and fighting with each other a lot, and it is driving her nuts. She is rarely consistent, and her general approach is to yell "stop it," followed by threats of punishment, which she occasionally carries out. Sometimes she and her husband waste an inordinate amount of time trying to find out who started the fight. Once in a while, one of the boys receives a spanking. Nothing seems to work. Mother and father sometimes argue in front of the kids about how to handle the current fight.

Behavior That Hurts

Because situations occur unexpectedly, parents generally react impulsively, out of frustration. They have no strategy regarding how to deal with them (e.g., what to ignore, what to address, how to respond in a more consistent manner, or how to prevent fights in the first place). Nagging, threatening, and punishing become repetitious and lead to escalation of frustrations, with everyone feeling more insecure.

Behavior That Helps

Parents need to recognize that what they are doing isn't working, and that they must do something different. They need to make a distinction between prevention and remediation, brainstorm new ways to deal with each, and agree on approaches that both can support consistently.

For example, to emphasize prevention:

1. Make expectations and consequences clear to the children (e.g., differences and conflict are acceptable, but hitting is unacceptable).

2. Have periodic family meetings to discuss such topics as why violence is unacceptable and alternative ways of handling frustrations.

3. Hold regular family feedback sessions, giving children and parents an outlet to talk out frustrations. (See Chapter 4, *Game Plan #3*.)

Remarks

◆ Not having a previously well-thought-out philosophy or strategy, parents often overreact, responding inconsistently in a mini-crisis atmosphere.

- Emphasis needs to be on prevention rather than correction.

- Include children in discussions of family values about aggressive behavior. This needs to begin early and be repeated periodically.

- Include children in establishing clear behavioral expectations and consequences for deviations.

- Expectations and consequences should be consistently adhered to and implemented with firmness, but not anger.

- When reasonable expectations and consequences are adhered to consistently by loving parents, children feel more secure.

- Providing non-aggressive outlets for expression of family member's feelings and frustrations contributes to prevention.

- Children should be praised when they work things out without fighting.

SITUATION 11: ACCEPTANCE, SECURITY
(Sex and the Pre-Teenager)

Six-year-old Kathy was dropped off by her mother at a neighbor's house early Saturday morning to spend a day with a school friend. Late that afternoon, Mom picked up Kathy and, on the way home, asked her if she had had fun with her friend. Kathy mentioned that one of the highlights was watching a wonderful movie on TV. When she told her mom the name of the movie, the latter was surprised, knowing that it contained sexually explicit language and scenes. Soon after, she was aghast when Kathy at one point, in telling the story of the movie, said, ". . . then I think he sexed her in the back seat of the car." The startled mom gasped, "Oh!" and quickly changed the subject. A moment of panic set in. Reflecting on it later, she vowed to screen more carefully what Kathy watched and whose home she could visit.

Behavior That Hurts

Parental fears often cause an overreaction to things that happen with children. In this case, the mother was upset but did not act on her feelings. Some parents might have responded strongly, admonishing the child about watching such films or talking about sex as she had, the implication being that she did something wrong.

Behavior That Helps

When surprised by a child's action, and not sure what to do, the best thing is to say nothing, which is what the mom did in this case. The parent can let it go and wait until the subject of sex comes up again, or until the child shows curiosity or initiates questions. On the other hand, recognizing the statement by Kathy to be ambiguous, the parent can explore to find out what the child means (in a low-key manner). For example, "When you say he sexed her in the back seat, what did you mean by that?" can provide an opportunity to find out what Kathy knows, how she feels about what she knows, and a chance to develop healthy attitudes about sex. Rather than a danger, here was an opportunity to connect with her daughter about sex.

Remarks

- ◆ For the child's sense of security and their own, parents need to have a strategy for dealing confidently with sensitive or taboo subjects, such as sex, at a level appropriate to the child's maturity.

◆ If one accepts the notion of discussing sex with a child whenever the child raises the subject, or when the parent feels it may be timely, then parents need to be informed and prepared.

◆ Reading about the subject will enable parents to take advantage of opportunities to connect with children confidently whenever the occasion presents itself.

SITUATION 12: INCLUSION
(A Failure to Communicate!)

Parents complain to friends about the difficulty of getting their 9- and 12-year-old children to communicate with them. The mother gives, as a typical example, the following interaction when one of them returns from school. Mother asks, "How was school today?"

Child: "Okay."
Mom: "What did you do?"
Child: "Nothing."
Mom: "Did you have fun?"
Child: "No."
Mom: "How come?"
Child: "Boring."

Behavior That Hurts

The timing is poor. The child wants to change clothes and go out and play. The context for a real exchange is not favorable. The interaction is in an interview format, not an exchange. The child often feels that it is an interrogation. Questions are often mundane and posed in an unenthusiastic manner, while the parent is doing something else. The exercise is more like a perfunctory ritual that sometimes takes place between husband and wife in marriages that have gone stale.

Behavior That Helps

Parents need to avoid squeezing in conversations on the run, or when a child's mind is elsewhere; selecting a favorable time for conversations is more likely to achieve a desired result. Initiating conversations where there is already initial interest would be helpful (e.g., a movie that kids are talking about, something going on in the family or in the parent's own life, or a hot topic currently in the news).

Remarks

♦ Parents need to recognize and avoid repetitive, perfunctory, ritualistic conversations and talk about things of real interest.

♦ Set aside regular times for discussions (e.g., mealtimes, after dinner).

♦ Discuss things in your life that might be of interest to the children or current newspaper stories or films that relate to events in their lives to stimulate conversation.

SITUATION 13: ACCEPTANCE, SECURITY
(Better Late Than Never—or Is It?)

A teenage son was out to a party with friends on a Saturday night. His mother had requested him to be home by midnight. He didn't get home until an hour later. When he arrived home, he started to apologize, but his mother interrupted, shouting that she had been "worried to death," that it was inexcusable he hadn't called to say he would be late, and that he would be punished. He protested angrily that he had tried to call, but that the line was busy. She accused him of lying. He shouted back, "Stop treating me like a baby!" and stomped off to his room.

Behavior That Hurts

The mother's anger immediately put the boy on the defensive, and soon a conflict was underway, with each one matching the other's negative energy. She felt he was being thoughtless and insensitive to her concerns. He felt she was being hypocritical—if she had been "worried to death," why wasn't she happy or relieved to see him? Neither of them was able to see the situation from the other's viewpoint. Their emotions, and need to be right, kept them from a problem-solving approach; instead the situation escalated into a power struggle.

Behavior That Helps

Either one of them could have broken the cycle of matching each other's negative responses, and it could have been handled peacefully and agreeably. Ideally, the mother could have expressed her relief that he was okay and her concern caused by his not calling. She could have given him the benefit of the doubt about the phone call, hugged him, and sent him to bed. The next day they could have discussed how to prevent the situation from happening again. The son could have ignored his mother's initial anger and waited until she calmed down to apologize, and discuss what happened.

Remarks

◆ The parent's need for control and her anxiety came into conflict with the teenager's need for independence. Neither is able to think in terms of, "What can I do to help satisfy the other person's need, and possibly get what I want?" Emotion takes over. The result is that no one benefits—neither peace of mind or control for the parent, nor independence for the son.

◆ Because such situations constantly reappear in different shapes and forms, parents need to develop a constructive strategy for avoiding and resolving problems. For example, for particularly sensitive and recurring situations, mutually acceptable limits and consequences should be established in advance.

◆ These interactions should be handled with mutual respect, seeking remedies rather than trying to establish blame or win an argument.

SUMMING UP

In most of the situations described above, we find interactions governed more by emotions than rationality. Differences escalate, leaving parents and children feeling stressed and unfulfilled. The emphasis is frequently on being right and forcing the other person to see it, not on understanding and satisfying each other's needs.

In the course of a year, most situations recur in varying degrees and forms. If we face each one as if we have never encountered it before, we will continue to shoot from the hip. However, if our approach is directed toward satisfying the child's five critical needs, we will be able to act more confidently, consistently, and positively, irrespective of the particular nature of each situation.

We can learn from each situation by using the critical needs as a guide in asking such questions as:

What would I have liked to have happen in the situation?

What did I learn about my own needs, behavior, strengths, weaknesses, thoughts, and attitudes?

With the five critical needs in mind, what could I have done differently?

By so doing, we will become better students of our own behavior and more conscious and effective parents. We will approach situations, not as skirmishes to be won, but rather with the attitude that *every interaction with our children is an opportunity to teach and to learn, to connect or disconnect,* and with the intention of creating endless connections.

T H R E E

Recollections
From Childhood

(Memories Have Impact)

*A*s children, we are very impressionable. Our parents have a great impact on us. For most of our childhood, our very survival depends on them. They're the ones with whom we spend the most time and are most intimately and emotionally involved. Because they become our main role models, for better or for worse, their influence on us is significant, often lasting far into our adult years and frequently affecting how we raise our own children.

At the time of a parent's death, many people express regret that they had not gotten to know their parents better. Life is short, so start now. Children are eager to know what parents think and feel, and why they do some of the things they do. Greater awareness of the effect of parent behavior on their children could contribute to more conscious and improved parenting.

In Chapter 2, we gave examples of supportive and non-supportive parent behavior in regard to the five critical needs of children. In this chapter, "grown-ups" (teenagers through senior citizens) give first-hand recollections of their parents' behavior and how it affected whether or not they felt *respected, important, accepted, included,* or *secure* during childhood.

The statements below represent a sample of responses to a questionnaire completed by over 200 individuals, most of them following a lecture or seminar on parent-child relations given by the author.

The task posed in the questionnaire was the following:

In thinking about your relationship with your parents, indicate on the attached questionnaire examples of communication, behavior, actions, attitudes of your parents which might possibly have affected—positively or negatively—your feeling *respected, important, accepted, included,* or *secure* as you were growing up.

Selected Responses

RESPECT

Not Feeling Respected

1. When I experimented with clothes, my folks made fun of me.

2. I was constantly interrupted before I could finish my thoughts.

3. When my mother took me shopping for clothes, she would end up shouting at me in public because I didn't like what she wanted to get me. I felt humiliated.

4. Sometimes I was embarrassed by comments that were made about me in my presence, as though I weren't there.

5. They showed me off, wanted me to be impressive to other people, never asked if it was okay with me. When I balked, they were upset and called me stubborn.

6. When I was little, my mother changed my pants outdoors after I spilled something. I was embarrassed.

7. When someone asked me a question, my mother or father would jump in and answer for me. It was very annoying.

Feeling Respected

1. My mother never opened my mail—she always respected my privacy.

2. When we misbehaved, our parents did not yell, or call us names.

3. If I didn't want to eat something, I was not forced to as long as I would try it.

4. My father did not like how some of my friends dressed, but they never stopped me from inviting them to our home.

5. My mom would apologize for losing her temper with me and sometimes explained what set her off.

6. When an uncle made fun of my long hair and referred to me as a girl, my mother asked him not to do that.

7. My parents didn't nag me about doing my homework. They just asked me to let them know when it was done.

IMPORTANCE

Not Feeling Important

1. It seemed that I was frequently being told not to do something.

2. My father was an unhappy person. He would often tell me that I would never amount to anything. For a long time, I believed him.

3. When my sister had emotional problems, my parents never discussed it with me. Because she was ill, she got most of the attention. All through my childhood, I felt she was important and I wasn't.

4. We were never part of decision-making. For example, when we moved from Chicago to Tucson, my parents didn't ask our opinion or how we felt about changing schools.

5. When my mom got on the phone, my sister and I could not get her off to answer a question or talk to us; she was on the phone a lot.

6. When I placed second at a swim meet, my parents didn't seem enthusiastic and told me that I would have to work a lot harder to win. I was made to feel like a failure.

7. When I gave my opinion, my parents scornfully told me to keep quiet because I was too young to understand.

Feeling Important

1. They made time in their busy schedules to sit down and listen to me.

2. They occasionally shared with us what was going on in their lives.

3. Since I was a young child, I always worked in my father's office on weekends or vacation time. Although I started with simple tasks, I always felt very grownup to be allowed to spend time with my father in his world.

4. As an older sibling, my parents trusted me to watch over my sister as an early teen. They also allowed me to care for other young children and infants at an early age.

5. After my first semester at college, my parents let me prepare a budget for each semester. I had my own bank account and total control over all expenditures. They trusted that I would live within the budget and not confront them with emergencies.

6. My father worked at home as a cap-maker. I read articles to him from an adventure magazine while he worked. His enjoyment gave me a lot of pride and pleasure.

7. My parents gave me choices about clothes, food, friends, etc. When they didn't give me a choice, they explained why.

ACCEPTANCE

Not Feeling Accepted

1. When I displeased my mother, she'd say, "You're impossible. Why can't you be like your brother?"

2. When I decided I wanted to work after I finished school rather than go to college, I was made to feel like a failure.

3. I am 49 years old and my parents still criticize my decisions.

4. My parents always wanted to know about everything I was doing and were upset when I wouldn't tell them everything.

5. I felt as if my parents were always focusing on my faults. (My grandfather was an exception.)

6. Our parents never let us argue. They made us feel we were bad, rather than teach us how to argue.

7. Whenever I gave my father reasons for poor work in school, he would say he didn't want to hear excuses and wouldn't discuss it.

Feeling Accepted

1. My parents never objected to my inviting friends over, even when I didn't let them know in advance. Everyone was always welcome.

2. When I started to grow my hair long, I had a lot of trouble at school and with some of my relatives. My mom told me that it didn't really matter if my hair was long or short. It was what was inside a person that mattered.

3. I have always loved raw onions. No matter where we were, my mother always saw to it that I got raw onions with my hamburgers, hot dogs, corn flakes, or whatever.

4. They didn't try to talk me out of my career goal even though they weren't enthusiastic about it.

5. I was acknowledged by my mother for my ability to relate to, and be patient with, my elderly grandparents.

6. They rarely interfered with my selection of friends and activities.

7. My parents didn't get upset when I expressed strong opinions about things with which they disagreed; instead, they discussed them with me.

INCLUSION

Not Feeling Included

1. When my sister went to a community center for psychotherapy, my mother and father went, but I was left out.

2. My family was famous for protecting us from the truth. There were a lot of skeletons in the closet, which eventually everyone knew about but couldn't discuss.

3. Our family did very little together.

4. I was never asked how I felt about important things or how I felt after a big family argument. I was never able to listen to my parents discuss anything significant.

5. When I was 10 years old my mother remarried, but she never discussed it with my brothers and me beforehand.

6. I was never included when parents had company; I was always sent to my room.

7. I felt excluded from my father's life. I wonder if he would have acted differently had I not been a girl.

Feeling Included

1. I always looked forward to holidays, family excursions, and family get-togethers.

2. There were often family discussions where decisions would be made. Everyone was included, and I was always asked my opinion.

3. My mother shared some secrets with me. Sometimes she would involve me in selecting a gift for my father, and my name would be included on the card.

4. My father was a storyteller, and he would always oblige us when we asked for a "yarn." The stories were usually about his childhood, and he shared how he felt in many different situations.

5. Every Sunday morning my parents would read the paper in bed. We used to climb into the bed, and Dad would read us the comics, especially "Lil' Abner." It always ended with a "tickle-fight."

6. We did everything (well, almost everything) as a family. Every night during the workweek, before going to sleep, we would play card games. My father would often play checkers with me and later chess.

7. We did volunteer work together in community projects.

SECURITY

Not Feeling Secure

1. My parents' divorce was devastating, especially since they never discussed it adequately with us.

2. Constantly being criticized by my parents was unsettling.

3. My mother always seemed worried about money. Although we never discussed details, I felt we couldn't afford anything. I felt guilty every time I asked for anything.

4. Our parents fought a great deal, with a lot of anger; we didn't ever get to see them make up. It left a lasting mark on us.

5. Mom was out of the house a lot. We didn't feel she was around much.

6. My mom always said she was fat and ugly, so I thought I was too, since people said I looked like her.

7. I was always afraid to talk to my parents about any troubles I had, because they would become very upset, and I did not receive the support I needed.

Feeling Secure

1. No matter how bad their finances were, my parents never complained and always seemed happy. Growing up, I felt sorry for the poor children who lived around us, and it wasn't until I was fully grown that I realized we were no better off financially than they were.

2. My mother always made me feel better when I was sick or when I was scared. Even when I got into trouble, I always felt secure because I knew she cared.

3. Someone was always at home when I was there—if not my parents, extended family members were around. I grew up in a very stable neighborhood.

4. One of my parents read to me every night when I went to bed, and both of them always began and ended each day with warm hugs.

5. My parents were divorced when I was seven. Neither of them let us feel less because of it. They never talked badly about each other and were always cordial in our presence. They explained what happened without laying blame, and also made sure to emphasize that nothing was our fault.

6. My mother and father gave a lot to each other. I saw them as kind, tender, loving, very understanding, and deeply in love with each other. This was very reassuring.

7. Our parents never yelled or spanked us when we did something wrong; they'd take time to discuss it with us. Consequently, a disapproving look from either of our parents made a strong impression.

SUMMING UP

Parents are frequently unaware of the impact that things they say or do have on their children. Years later, adults vividly remember the effect on them of certain aspects of their parents' behavior. In fact, they may be doing some of the same things with their own children without realizing it. One way to find out, and start doing something about it, is for parents to use the positive and negative actions cited above under each of the five critical needs as a checklist. By checking every statement that applies to them, the result would be a list of behaviors they would want to either start or stop doing. This would be an initial agenda for more conscious and effective parenting.

As parents, we need to become more conscious students of our own behavior (see Chapter 4, *Game Plan #2*) and pay attention to the quality of our interactions with our children in relation to satisfying their needs. We also need to ask our children questions to learn more about how we are impacting them. Children's fears and concerns often go unexpressed or misinterpreted.

We need to share more of ourselves with our children, so they will learn how to share more with us, will want to share more, and will not fear to do so.

FOUR

Becoming a
Professional at Parenting

*(Childrearing Is
Too Important to
Leave to Chance)*

When interviewing parents for this book, I would ask them, "Do you agree with the following two statements: *Parenting is one of the most important responsibilities any of us can have in a lifetime. Parenting is also one of the most difficult, stressful, anxiety-provoking, and complex responsibilities anyone can ever have?*" The response to both was universally, "Yes." I would follow-up by asking, "How often do you and your spouse set time aside to ask the question, *How well are we doing as parents, and what could we be doing differently or better?*" The answer invariably was "Never."

Think about this response—quite a paradox, isn't it? By our own admission, parenting probably is the most important and most difficult responsibility anyone of us might have in a lifetime. Yet, it's rare that parents set aside time to question how well they are doing. Apparently parenting is something we do and not something we think about.

Later, when I would ask parents how they went about satisfying their children's emotional needs, the typical response was a perplexed: "What needs?" It felt as if I were speaking a foreign language. And I was. None of the parent responses surprised me. When my son was growing up, I would have responded the same way. Who knew? Nobody talked about emotional needs or health—not then and not now, not at home and not at school. That's why I call it the "missing agenda."

In the first three chapters, you have gained an understanding of the five critical emotional needs of children—what they are, why they are important, how they have been neglected, and ways in which parents can satisfy these needs. In this chapter, we will explore how parents can approach their responsibilities and implement the concepts in a more conscious and thoughtful manner as a way to eliminate the "missing agenda."

Amateur vs. Professional

In this section, I use the term "amateur" in the general sense of words such as beginner, naive, or inexperienced and "professional" as experienced, knowledgeable, and systematic.

Most parents are amateurs when it comes to parenting—that is, our behavior, both in quantity and in quality, belies the high priority we ascribe to child rearing. Our approach is hit or miss rather than systematic, reactive rather than proactive. There is nothing wrong with being an amateur. That's the way we all start out—untrained, inexperienced, unskilled—but hopefully with love in our hearts and a strong desire to learn and improve. The importance of parenting necessitates that we develop the expertise and systematic, conscious behavior of the professional, while conserving the love, enthusiasm, and spontaneity of the amateur. Without the qualities of the amateur, the professional can become cold and mechanical. Without the qualities of the professional, the amateur can become stumbling and ineffective.

Parenting is too important and complex to leave to chance. Given the goal of developing emotionally healthy children, a more professional approach will increase the probability of doing so and will additionally contribute to the emotional health of the parent. To remain amateurs means to continue a random approach, which results in inconsistency, unnecessary stress, and frustration for both child and parent. As amateurs, some parents succeed better than others, but all are underachievers in regard to what they could accomplish.

Elements of Professionalism

Becoming professional means becoming a conscious parent—that is, possessing a set of core values and applying them to parenting in a systematic and consistent way. The following discussion involves four essential elements of professionalism:

1. Making conscious decisions

2. Having a game plan

3. Becoming a student of one's own behavior

4. Having an experimental attitude

MAKING CONSCIOUS DECISIONS

The most consistent and predictable characteristic of contemporary society is change. Things are changing so rapidly that most of us are repeatedly brought up short by new circumstances. Pressures on families are strong. If parents do not focus on the family, children will be neglected.

Since change is inevitable, we have to decide whether to be a victim of forced change, which is what amateurs do, or become professionals and be part of planned change. Amateurs wait and let things happen. Professionals make conscious decisions and make things happen.

Planned change begins with a conscious decision by parents as to what they want their family life to be like. This is translated into goals and priorities which is the point of departure for developing plans.

HAVING A GAME PLAN

Without planning, a conscious decision or goal can be nothing but wishful thinking or lip service, like a New Year's resolution made on January 1st, which is a distant memory one or two weeks later.

A game plan, very simply, is a statement of the need to accomplish a goal. It can be simple or complex as required by the situation. A simple plan might be to prepare a schedule for reading this book—time and place (involves only yourself). Establishing a parent support group would be more complex (involves numbers of parents, initial meetings, and regularly scheduled ones, arrangements for procedures, time, place).

If you don't know where you are going, there's no telling where you'll wind up. If you know where you are going and have no plan to get there, you might not.

BECOMING A STUDENT OF YOUR
OWN BEHAVIOR

Most of us are very good students of other people's behavior. We know exactly what others should do to make things better. Husbands know just how wives should change to make the marriage better; wives know the same regarding their husbands; children and parents could each give the other advice on what to do differently—equally so for employers and employees. And so it goes throughout society—if only other people would do things differently, we think the world and our lives would be so much better.

Most of us are not very good students of our own behavior; rarely do we consider this as a goal, let alone a priority. Yet we know it is very difficult, if not impossible, to change another's behavior. The one you have most control over is yourself, and changes in one's own behavior can have positive effects on others. Thus, in any relationship where the results are not what you would like, your point of departure must be that you, not the other person, must do something different. Common sense tells us why. If you are not getting what you want, then clearly whatever you have been doing to that point is not working. For example, if nagging and threatening for several years has not gotten your child to keep his room clean, then you need to do something different rather than to persist in ineffective, self-defeating behavior.

If we considered ourselves a corporation—John Doe, Inc.—wouldn't we want to regularly take stock of our assets and liabilities, our strengths and our weaknesses, and attempt to build on the strengths and overcome the weaknesses? Otherwise, our weaknesses and liabilities could take over and cause us to go bankrupt. The high rate of divorce is an indication of how many marital relationships do go bankrupt, in which case the penalties paid by children are severe. As parents, we are engaged in developing the most precious commodity of all—our children. Nowhere is there a greater need to become a student of one's own behavior than in parenting.

HAVING AN EXPERIMENTAL ATTITUDE

From one point of view, it can be argued that life is nothing but one big experiment, and all of society represents a wonderful laboratory for us to try things, especially regarding family life.

Recognizing this and consciously adopting an experimental attitude has many benefits. With an experimental attitude, there is no such thing as failure. You never let yourself become a victim. If something isn't working the way you want it to, you don't wring your hands and say, "Poor me! Why is this happening? What did I do to deserve this?" As an experimenter, you say, "What am I going to try now to make it work?" You adopt the cliché, "If at first you don't succeed, try, try again," but you add what most people omit, "but each time in a different way." If you keep repeating something that isn't working, why would you expect the result to be different? In this case, practice does not make perfect. If you are practicing mistakes, you will get better and better at making mistakes. This is why many individuals do not become more effective at parenting through experience and why so many other relationships struggle.

With an experimental attitude, problems and difficulties become challenges. Each day affords the opportunity to use this wonderful laboratory called *life* to try something new. Parenting becomes a continuous, conscious experiment, a source of challenge and fascination to be savored.

Applying Elements of Professionalism

MAKING CONSCIOUS DECISIONS

When parents possess a clear set of core values, they are less likely to work at cross-purposes or to misunderstand each other's actions or motives. It gives focus to their parenting activities and increases the probability that they will act more effectively.

The initial step in making the five critical needs of children an effective part of family life is to solidify this intent with the following conscious decisions:

Adopting the Five Critical Needs

I will adopt the five critical needs as core values to guide my behavior as follows:

1. By treating my children with as much respect as I would want to receive and give.

2. By treating my children in ways that enhance their feeling of being important.

3. By accepting my children as unique, independent individuals entitled to their own ideas, feelings, thoughts, and opinions.

4. By helping my children feel a sense of community—creating family activities in which they are involved and viewing our family as a "Learning Community."

5. By increasing my children's feeling of security through role-modeling a loving, respectful relationship with my spouse or, if a single parent, with the significant others in my life.

HAVING A GAME PLAN

Changing habits or starting new habits is not easy. Many good intentions break down because they never get converted to action. The suggested game plans presented below are designed to facilitate the transition from concept to action.

This is not a definitive list or a one-size-fits-all approach. It is presented to stimulate your thinking and to provide alternatives to choose from, adopt, or modify. It is anticipated that you will create your own game plans appropriate to the needs of your family.

The idea is to make a commitment and get started immediately, even if only in a small way. Start with one game plan and build on this. It's better to get started in a limited way, rather than to wait until you can do it all and perhaps not do anything. As you gradually start doing things in a more systematic way, it will become easier and you will want to do more. Presented below are a variety of game plans for consideration.

GAME PLAN #1: Ongoing Review of Basic Concepts

Professional athletes and artists practice the basics of their profession before each game or event—tennis players warm up before a match, practicing basic strokes; baseball players do infield and batting drills; musicians tune their instruments. Parents can't exactly replicate the above before meeting their children each day, but they can review the basic concepts of the five critical needs of children regularly as follows:

Goal and Actions

To keep the basic concepts of the five critical needs fresh as a daily guide to interactions with our children. Choose from the following actions as necessary.

Weekly: Reread the *Summing Up* sections of Chapter 1, which summarize the rationale and importance of each of the five critical needs.

Quarterly: Reread Chapter 1. Review other chapters as needed.

GAME PLAN #2: Becoming A Student of
Your Own Behavior

Personal growth does not occur in a vacuum. We need to know how well we are doing—what's working and what's not—in order to make appropriate changes and adjustments. Professional athletes are fortunate in having objective data in the form of game and personal performance results. They also have the advantage of reviewing film and feedback from coaches and trainers. It is difficult for parents to get similar objective feedback. Nevertheless, recognizing these limitations, parents can begin to become students of their own behavior by keeping a daily journal, participating in family feedback sessions, requesting feedback from one's spouse and children in one-on-one situations, and starting or joining a parent support group.

Goal

To better understand how my behavior affects my children and to facilitate my efforts to satisfy their emotional needs.

Actions

1. Keep a daily journal by taking 15-20 minutes at the end of each day to reflect on the questions below. (Answer each question briefly using Appendix C—*Becoming a Student of My Own Behavior* form.)

    ◆ Which of my actions helped to satisfy any of my children's five critical needs?

    ◆ Which of my actions detracted from satisfying any of the five needs?

    ◆ What did I learn about myself—attitudes, behavior, strengths, weaknesses?

    ◆ If I did today over, what would I change?

◆ Questions I have about my children's or my attitudes and behavior are?

Remarks

Keeping such a journal—even for one month—will greatly surprise you as to how much you learn about yourself and your children, and how useful the information can be. An adjunct to this activity would be an end-of-week discussion by parents of content from their daily journals. This activity alone can have a profound effect on the quality of the interactions with your children and the sense of confidence in what you are doing.

GAME PLAN #3: Family Feedback

Family feedback sessions are an ongoing form of family meetings. These provide a regular forum for creating a safe, non-threatening atmosphere for open communication to take place; they provide an outlet for feelings, concerns, frustrations, appreciations, and joy. It is a sharing and learning situation where everyone receives information about what's going on with one another, and how one's actions might be affecting other family members.

Goal

To improve family relations through feedback sessions.

Actions

1. Initial Meeting: Parents discuss purpose of meeting— i.e., to find out how everyone is doing so they can remove obstacles and make suggestions for leading happy, healthy lives together. Ground rules include: one person speaks at a time, no interruptions, everyone has equal permission to say anything.

2. Ongoing Weekly Sessions: the following open-ended questions are addressed in these sessions.

   ◆ What do we see one another or ourselves doing that is getting in the way or helping us to lead happy, healthy lives?

   ◆ What do we like most or least about our family life?

   ◆ What else is going on in our lives that is causing us to feel good, bad, concerned, relaxed, or appreciative?

   ◆ What could we be doing to make things better?

3. Parents set tone:

   ◆ Initially, parents may want to start sessions with a request for feedback to set the tone—"What have I done this past week that you liked or didn't like?"

   ◆ To make it safe for children to respond honestly, parents need to be accepting of comments, and to emphasize that there will be no negative consequences for anything said.

   ◆ Some families might begin with a round robin with each member taking 1-2 minutes to mention one's own highlights and lowlights for the past week, before engaging in feedback.

(See Appendix D—*Family Feedback Critique Form* to use for above notes.)

Remarks

Giving and receiving honest feedback and open communication is not easy for most people. It may take a while for these sessions to become habitual, but gradually sessions will be easier and benefits will become obvious. You should not rush the process. Although talking about frustrations and offering criticism is part of feedback, so is appreciating the things people feel good about. When matters come up that need problem solving, follow-ups outside the meeting can take place. Sessions may vary in frequency from weekly to once or twice a month, and in length from 30 minutes to one hour or more (weekly meetings generally work best). Both frequency and length of sessions will depend on the size and needs of the family and may change over time. Family feedback sessions afford an opportunity for parents and children to get to know and understand one another and themselves better, and become more effective in satisfying one another's emotional needs.

GAME PLAN #4: Emphasizing Positive
                         Reinforcement

Parents tend to pay more attention to kids when they misbehave than when they are doing things right. Kids are generally subject to much more criticism than praise, and this can have a negative effect on their self-image and confidence. Children need more positive feedback.

Goal

To provide a child with an abundance of positive feedback.

Actions

1. Provide a special day, and decide on the time of day for the meeting, length of time, and place.

2. Give the day a name such as Positive Monday (or whatever the day of the week is).

3. Observe child's actions with the goal of acknowledging praiseworthy behavior. Praise should be for specific

behavior appropriate to the child's actions (e.g., neither phony, nor exaggerated).

4. Children can participate by giving praise to each other and to parents.

5. Experiment with the way praise is given.

Remarks

Through this activity, parents frequently discover more positive behavior than they might have expected. Parents should remember that praise must be sincere and deserved— "make-believe" will not work. But it can be for any act, no matter how small; e.g., saying hello to someone with a big cheerful smile. One parent created a game with her son in which either one could initiate a positive interaction by saying, "I have a compliment for you when you have a compliment for me." When the second person is ready, the two exchange compliments. The reciprocal nature of this activity enables the child to not only experience the satisfaction of being acknowledged, but also of providing that pleasure for someone else.

GAME PLAN #5: Planning a Family Activity

Many parents engage in activities with children that are fun and interesting for the kids, but perhaps boring to the adults. Of course, the pleasure is in seeing the kids enjoying themselves or learning something. Parents will always be involved in a certain number of these activities. However, there are many activities the whole family can enjoy. When such activities accomplish a needed task, are fun for everyone, provide some learning, and give the kids a feeling of inclusion, you are accomplishing many things at once.

Goal

To create a family activity which promotes feelings of inclusion and importance for the children—garage sale/house-uncluttering project.

Actions

1. Initial family meeting: Involve everyone in a meeting where the project is described and tasks, responsibilities, and income sharing are agreed upon, and completion dates for each activity described below are specified.

2. Making a list of things to sell: Each person independently makes a list of things to sell by answering the following questions:

   ◆ What things of my own do I want to sell?

   ◆ What are some things in the house that I don't like?

   ◆ What are some things that nobody seems to use?

   ◆ What are some things that I haven't worn or used in over a year?

   ◆ What are some things I'm not sure I want to keep?

3. One or two persons are assigned to combine each person's selections into a master list, eliminating duplication.

4. Family meeting to arrive at a consensus on the final sale list.

5. Subsequent meeting(s) to plan the details of the sale—who does what, where, when, and how.

Remarks

The project does not have to be for conducting a garage sale. The purpose could be just to unclutter the house, and items could be given to charity. Additional benefits might involve having children participate in delivering the items, and perhaps learning something about the receiving charity. A family party might be a fun conclusion to such a project. Other family activities/projects with similar goals could take place periodically. (See Appendix A—*Guide to Parent Resources,* Lewis, B. A., *The Kids Guide to Service Projects.*)

In addition to feeling included and important, children learn planning, problem solving, conversation, and teamwork skills.

GAME PLAN #6: Establishing Family Rules

Children feel more secure when they know what's expected of them, and where parent reactions are consistent and not subject to whims or moods. When rules are well thought out and involve input from the children, they are more likely to be accepted.

Parents frequently avoid such discussions because they feel more comfortable exercising adult control. They are sometimes fearful of getting involved in endless debates where they might "give in to the kids." This again is operating out of fear. Yes, as kids grow older, they desire more power and independence, but parents should welcome this rather than fear it. Insecurity often leads to fear of losing control and the exercise of arbitrary power. This promotes endless conflict. Along with the desire for independence, kids have a strong need to please their parents and can be reasonable. Parents should help them by role-modeling rational discussion, decision-making, compromise, and cooperation.

Goal

To develop rules/guidelines of behavior for the family through the mechanism of shared planning and decision-making.

Actions

1. Initial family meeting: Discuss the family unit as a microcosm of society in which mutual respect and cooperation are necessary for growth, happiness, and security. Discuss the five critical needs as a basic family value governing their interaction with one another.

2. Follow-up meeting(s):

   ◆ Briefly discuss (not all at one meeting) family values in relation to learning/education, health, work, interpersonal relations, etc.

   ◆ Use family values as a context to discuss the need for rules—for homework, television, computer, telephone, meals, bedtime, fighting, chores, as well as behavior outside the home—also, to learn about and develop skills in negotiation and compromise. Seek consensus with children on rules and consequences. Adopt only a few at first. Start with the most necessary rules first. You can always add more rules later.

   ◆ Periodic meetings are held to monitor how things are going and to make changes where necessary.

Remarks

This activity can go a long way to eliminate emotional conflict and patterns of nagging, threats, punishment, frustration, and submission. It should be stressed that the initial plan is the family's best thinking at a given moment in time, and that there will be ongoing evaluation. This activity can and should begin at an early age. To become skilled at participating in democratic environments and to appreciate their value, children need to experience them first hand, something which is not possible in autocratic families and schools. (A by-product can be improved skills in reading, writing, listening, speaking, problem solving, compromising, researching.)

It should be made clear that every decision will not involve consensus seeking, and in all cases, parents remain the final authority.

GAME PLAN #7: Creating Family Traditions

The breakdown of the American family—currently a worrisome concern permeating all segments of society—needs to be addressed by every family.

Goal

To create events that combine elements of fun, interest, and learning that are repeated on a regular basis so as to become family traditions.

Actions

1. Parents discuss with children their intention to create special event evenings, and/or weekends, which would take place on a regular basis, frequency, and time to be decided.

2. Family brainstorms ideas. For example:

    ◆ Comedy evenings. Each one brings in a joke to tell or a funny story to read.

    ◆ Question and answer evenings. Each person makes up one question or selects from a book such as Stock's *The Kids Book of Questions.* Each person then asks a question followed by family discussion.

    ◆ Gift-giving project, to encourage the concept that "it's better to give than to receive," or at least as important. Throughout the year, on occasions where people usually give gifts, involve the children in some way as a giver.

Remarks

Many families already engage in certain traditions. With a little thought, new ones can be added or used to replace existing ones. Many traditions continue throughout the children's growing-up years and sometimes beyond. (See Appendix B—*Family Activities List,* for over 150 categories of potential family activities.)

GAME PLAN #8: Family Reading/Storytelling Activity

One of the fond memories many people have of childhood is having parents read to them or tell them a story before going to bed. My father was a great storyteller, and it is something that became a ritual with me and my son. Each day would end with his getting into bed and my telling him a bedtime story and giving him a goodnight hug and kiss. This activity has become a tradition in many families, but not as many as one might hope. It is an excellent parent-child activity to end the day, providing comfort and pleasure to the child, along with motivation to read or improve learning skills. Also, it can serve as a signal for bedtime and a transition to prepare the child for it.

Goal

Establish reading as an important activity through a pleasurable and peaceful end-of-day parent-child interaction.

Actions

1. Start this activity as early as infancy, first with storytelling and then with reading from books. Librarians can recommend books that are popular at each age level.

2. Families with more than one child occasionally can have all participate at one time, with children taking turns reading or older ones reading to younger ones.

Remarks

At one elementary school, the principal held a daily reading hour in order to emphasize the importance of reading. Everyone in the school—students, teachers, administrators, office, and maintenance staff—stopped whatever they were doing and read for 45 minutes. This was followed by small group discussions. The interest level in this activity was high. As children get older, this can become a weekly family activity, perhaps with everyone occasionally reading the same book.

GAME PLAN #9: A Team Approach to Cooking
and Kitchen Work

Parents can get more mileage out of family projects by undertaking some that are useful to all members. Kitchen activities around the preparation of meals offer such possibilities, especially because it is something that takes place several times each day and is an activity in which all people participate throughout their lives.

Goal

To create a mini-culinary school that will provide children with gradually increasing responsibilities, skills, and appreciation of food.

Actions

1. Outline a brief curriculum for the gradual training of children in all tasks related to preparing and serving meals.

2. List tasks from simple to complex so as to be able to involve children at all ages (e.g., handing things to cook from refrigerator; setting table; opening cans; maintenance tasks such as cleaning table, putting things away,

washing dishes, drying dishes, sweeping the floor; taking out the garbage; preparing vegetables; preparing
simple snacks and dishes such as hors d'oeuvres, cold
sandwiches, cold and warm cereal, hard-boiled eggs,
baked potatoes; making menu suggestions; preparing
menus for different meals; serving guests; making a
shopping list; assisting parent with shopping; doing
shopping alone; simple and advanced cooking).

3. Assign tasks to children and titles (e.g., assistant chef,
    maintenance manager, chief food taster).

4. Provide on-the-job instruction prior to performing each
    task.

Remarks

As children learn to do more and become more useful, it
will contribute to their confidence and independence and
help to lessen the parents' workload, which is especially
important with single-parent families or where both parents
work.

GAME PLAN #10: Family Study of Respect—
Meaning and Significance

Children learn from role models. They can learn what to do
and what not to do if they see enough of it, know what they
are looking for, and can recognize and understand why something is positive or negative.

Goal

To create a deeper understanding of, and preference for, respectful behavior through active observation and discussion.

Actions

1. Parents discuss purpose of activity and define respectful and disrespectful behavior, using examples from Chapter 1.

2. During a specified period (e.g., one week), each person makes notes of examples of disrespectful and respectful behavior at one or more of the following locations: at school, play, home, television. At the end of the week, the family meets to discuss results of observations and conclusions.

Remarks

This activity may be conducted at different intervals throughout the year. It provides another opportunity for parents to share their values with the children. From time to time, children and parents take note of their own acts of respect or disrespect and discuss them together.

GAME PLAN #11: Parent Self-Care

To create a positive, happy, relaxed family atmosphere, parents need to avoid the burnout pitfall—that is, being so involved in the care of their children that they neglect their own needs. When this happens, parents lack energy, feel less joy, experience much stress, and are not as effective with their children. Parents need to nourish themselves as well as their children.

Goal

To identify activities that will satisfy parents' personal needs and prepare a plan to implement them.

Actions

1. Review areas of personal pursuits such as socializing, exercising, sports, travel, hobbies, learning, reading, volunteering, and so on, and identify those activities which would be high-priority choices.

2. Think about how much time you now spend in personal pursuits—alone or with others, time spent, and with whom. (See Appendix E—*Parent Self-Care Plan Form* to use for this survey.)

3. With the information from #1 and #2 above, prepare a tentative plan for a period of time (e.g., six months) to schedule the high-priority activities identified in #1 and #2 above.

4. Weekly: Evaluate extent to which self-care plan is working. (See Appendix F—*Parent Self-Care Evaluation Form* to use for this activity.)

5. Yearly: When possible, prepare plan for six months or one year.

Remarks

Parents usually have a limited amount of time for personal pursuits—all the more reason to make conscious decisions about spending leisure time alone, with your spouse, and with friends, and selecting activities you would enjoy.

Because self-care is an area that parents many times neglect, having a plan adds focus and increases the probability of it occurring. As parents become better students of their own behavior, adjustments can be made to come up with a realistic, balanced approach. (As time is frequently a major problem, read or re-read Chapter 5 on *Overcoming Obstacles . . .*)

GAME PLAN #12: Participating in a
Parent Support Group

Parents can enlarge their vision of parenting and get practical support by meeting with other parents on a regular basis to share experiences, solve problems, exchange feedback, and support one another in numerous other ways.

Goal

To create a support group of parents interested in helping one another become more effective parents, with less stress, and more joy.

Actions

1. One or more parents invite others to a meeting to discuss the purpose and procedures of such a group, and to establish a regular schedule for getting together.

2. Group can start with as few as two or three members and should not wait to recruit some arbitrary number of persons.

3. In addition to sharing ideas and experiences, other activities from which most parents can benefit include babysitting, sharing transportation, telephone hotline, trading children's clothing, loaning equipment, cooperative nursery, tutoring, exchanging books, etc.

Remarks

Parents who have participated in such groups have indicated that members become close and frequently function like an extended family. Many have found that the group helped reduce stress and contributed to their becoming better parents.

BECOMING A STUDENT OF YOUR OWN BEHAVIOR

Previously we discussed why feedback was important and the negative consequences caused by its absence. Here we will address potential problems and solutions in implementing feedback activities and suggestions for getting off to a good start.

I will begin with two true stories that are relevant to this discussion. A friend was attending his mother's 80th birthday celebration when she approached him and asked for the first time, "Son, was I a good mother?" Surprised by her question, he looked at her, smiled, and said, "Mom, you're the best."

At one of my workshops a childcare provider related how, immediately after reading *How to Raise Emotionally Healthy Children,* she met with her two sons, ages 7 and 10, and asked, "Do I treat you boys with respect?" The younger boy looked at her with a funny expression and said, "Sure, Mom," and then skipped away. The 10-year-old looked straight at her and said emphatically, "Not always." The parent gasped and then asked for an example. To which he replied, "Sometimes you're sarcastic." "I am?" she asked, with a tone of disbelief. And then Mom asked him to be more specific. He proceeded to describe coming to her a few days earlier in the kitchen, asking for help, and her shouting at him, "Can't you see I only have two hands?" Embarrassed, she apologized and remarked that because she's not always aware of how she comes across, to please let her know the next time something like that happens.

The two situations above are illustrative of a resource—the family itself—that can help parents become better students of their own behavior. However, asking one another for feedback is rare among family members, nor does it occur to parents to have regular family feedback sessions to talk about what's happening in their lives and how to make them better.

How to Raise Emotionally Healthy Children has awakened people to the possibilities.

The following are things to consider when engaging in such activities. Feedback is not a magic pill. You will need to work at it. Most of us find it difficult to accept criticism. From infancy on, we have been plagued by a non-stop barrage of warnings, corrections, and scoldings, at home and at school, leaving us insecure to varying degrees. To avoid reprimands or punishment, we have learned to be defensive and to lie. This is done without having consciously decided to do so.

With the above in mind, here are some suggestions for initiating feedback activities in families and getting the most benefit from them.

- Cultivate a positive attitude (all feedback is useful).

    - View criticism as an act of friendship and concern, not hostility.

    - Positive—Keep it up, expand on it if possible.

    - Critical—If you agree with it, use it to take positive action. If you disagree, take the opportunity to clarify and clear the air.

- Start with *Becoming Students of Own Behavior.* (See Game Plan #2.) (This involves only you with no one looking over your shoulder.)

- Join or start a parent support group at the earliest opportunity. (See Game Plan #12.) (A non-threatening opportunity to share similar life experiences with peers.)

- Two person feedback—start when you and your spouse feel comfortable after working with Game Plan #2. (Use Family Feedback approach. See Game Plan #3.)

- Start family feedback as soon as both parents feel comfortable. (See Game Plan #3.)

Engaging in the feedback activities described above has the potential for being one of the most interesting and valuable experiences of family life. However, if you became actively engaged in *Game Plan #2,* "Becoming A Student of Your Own Behavior," that in itself could have a profound effect on your effectiveness as a parent.

Note

If other types of family meetings have taken place, as discussed in Chapter 1, *Need to Feel Included,* it will facilitate starting the feedback meetings. Also, consider having teenagers and pre-teens read Chapter 1, and discuss with them the "five needs as a family value" prior to feedback.

HAVING AN EXPERIMENTAL ATTITUDE

Accepting life as one big experiment, the family becomes a fertile and special laboratory to conduct your very own research on how to create an emotionally healthy environment in which the individuals are both the experimenters and the subjects. My first recommendation is to think big! You can always act small later. Don't limit yourself in the thinking stage. Starting with wherever you are at this moment in time, and with whatever skills, talent, health, personalities, possessions, needs, and wants that you have, and begin a dialogue on how to grow happy, healthy, helpful people, individuals who can incorporate the five critical emotional needs into their lives.

A good place to start might be with "Becoming A Student of Your Own Behavior" because it doesn't require getting anyone else involved. As you refer to your Daily Journal and identify something you did well, you might then choose to try different ways to expand on this or, for something you didn't do well, ways to improve. Starting family meetings early in the process is important. This is where you emphasize the concept of the family as a community and what that means in terms of responsibilities to one another and for one's own well-being. All of the Game Plans are excellent opportunities for experimentation according to your needs, desires, and readiness. (See Appendices G—*Family Activities Plan,* H—*Family Activities Evaluation,* and I—*Children's Well-Being Survey.*)

Summing Up

It is ironic that as important as inter-personal relations, communication, and feedback are, nobody teaches us about any of this during our formative years—as with emotional health, they are not part of anyone's curriculum, neither at home nor at school. They are part of the *missing agenda.* Unfortunately, we pay a considerable price for this void throughout our lives, but it doesn't have to be that way.

In this chapter, we stressed the importance of becoming a conscious, thoughtful parent, of not leaving parenting to chance. The goal of developing emotionally healthy children involves making your child's emotional needs a priority, applying the four elements of professionalism as a strategy, and maintaining a balanced lifestyle by not neglecting your own personal needs.

The game plans in this chapter are not intended as panaceas. They are models that parents can adopt, modify, or use to create new ones. Given the multiple demands and pressures on parents, becoming a professional at parenting does not mean doing everything at once. A suggested basic program of initial activities is to:

(1) Read the book—once through rapidly—and then re-read Chapters 1 and 4.

(2) Start applying the five needs in everyday interactions with the children.

(3) Become a student of your own behavior by keeping a daily journal.

(4) As soon as it is feasible, participate in a parent support group. Subsequent activities can be undertaken at any time a parent feels ready and motivated and the situation makes it practical.

In addition to satisfying children's five critical needs and strengthening family cohesion, there are important potential by-products from these activities. These include improving children's reading, writing, speaking, and thinking skills. They also provide opportunities for fun, relaxation, challenge, and experimentation.

Individuals, like organizations, must continually be able to adapt to change and renew themselves. This is particularly true in contemporary society, and for the foreseeable future, where the most constant and predictable characteristic is change. A strategy for self-renewal and self-correction helps us to confront change and adapt to new conditions. Applying the four elements of professionalism—making conscious decisions, having a game plan, being a student of your own behavior, having an experimental attitude—provides a framework for parents to satisfy children's five critical needs and strengthen family cohesion in a positive, consistent, and efficient manner.

FIVE

Overcoming Obstacles and Taking Control

(Maintaining Focus and a Balanced Lifestyle)

*W*ith what you now know, it's time to move ahead confidently, from talk to action—implementing the concepts and reaping the benefits for children, parents, families, schools, and society at large. However, not so fast. With any endeavor—no matter how well we may know what needs to be done—there are always obstacles to succeeding, sometimes internal where we get in our own way and sometimes unforeseen external factors. The intention of this chapter is to anticipate many of these potential difficulties and suggest ways to avoid or overcome them.

Obstacles

FEELING OVERWHELMED

A common problem that parents often speak about is stress—that is, having feelings of being overwhelmed, of being frustrated or worn out. The question frequently asked, with an overtone of helplessness, is: "Where do I find the time to do everything I have to do?" As one mother said, "How can I implement all these wonderful ideas when sometimes I can't even find time to prepare a proper meal or do the laundry?" When both parents work, or in the case of a single parent, the problems are further exacerbated.

In addition to the actual amount of work involved in parenting, a considerable amount of energy often goes into worry. Golda Meier, former prime minister of Israel, wrote in her autobiography about the worry, guilt and stress she experienced because of the conflicting demands of work and family. When at work she worried about her kids, when at home she worried about her work. In such situations, some amount of worry is inevitable. However, it is not in our own or our children's best interest to become overwhelmed by such worry—much better to do something about it.

LACK OF PLANNING

Common sense tells us that when you have more to do than time available, something must give. What gets neglected should not be left to chance. It should be a conscious decision. If not, you will continue to feel overwhelmed because of all the things you don't get done, even though there was no way to have done them in the first place. Sometimes the kids are victims of this neglect, other times it is the parents, but in either case it is the family as a whole that suffers.

RESISTANCE TO PLANNING

Planning involves establishing goals and priorities, assigning responsibilities, allocating time, simplifying one's life, making conscious choices. This type of planning is not rocket science—effective parents do it intuitively—but all too often, it does not happen. Some of the reasons for this are described below.

Cultural Conditioning

Our culture generally values *doing* rather than *thinking* or *planning*. As a consultant to schools and corporations, I would often hear an administrator or executive at a planning meeting state that the meeting should be cut short so everyone could get back to work. Planning was not considered work. A common complaint is that meetings waste time, but we know that purposeful, well-organized meetings save time. In fact, the busier you are, the more carefully you have to plan—although it takes time, it saves much more. Nevertheless, as one parent said, "I don't have time to plan. I'm too far behind already."

Myth of Spontaneity

There is also what I call *the myth of spontaneity*. Some people feel constrained by a plan or a schedule. They place a high value on being spontaneous and feel locked in by structure. But without a plan, important things are sometimes neglected and lesser ones get done. Also, consistency, which is important to children, is sacrificed. The purpose of planning is to insure that the things we say are important actually do occur, and in a timely and consistent manner.

Planning is not incompatible with spontaneity, inspiration or intuition. If anything occurs that makes us want to deviate, we should remember it is *our* plan and we can do what we want. In fact, having a plan facilitates spontaneity, since we have the security of a structure to return to.

The famous Russian theater director, Stanislavski, once cautioned actors that since inspiration occurred so rarely, it was essential to master the basics. This underlines a misconception about how artists and other creative people work—far from being undisciplined, they are among the most disciplined persons we know. When someone once asked the famous composer, Hindermith, when he composed, he replied, "From nine to five."

Advantages of Being Overwhelmed

As much as we may protest and complain about being overwhelmed, I believe that many of us unconsciously keep ourselves in this position because of hidden benefits. For one thing, it enables a parent to feel like a martyr and to evoke sympathy. People are less likely to place demands on us if we are overwhelmed. It makes us less accountable when we make mistakes or forget to do something. After all, what can anyone expect, given how overwhelmed we are. Sometimes, because of this, we unconsciously subvert our own efforts to plan, to get organized, to make things work.

OVER-SERIOUSNESS

We parents tend to take everything too seriously, especially ourselves. This tendency probably reaches its height with the arrival of our first child but does not ever completely go away. We agonize over decisions as though our child's life depended on each one. We are sometimes conscientious to a fault. If things are going okay today, we'll worry about tomorrow. If we could, we would live our children's lives for them, attempting to spare them any suffering. In the process, we create a heavy atmosphere and sometimes become a burden to ourselves and to our children.

We need to lighten up, cut the drama and move to joy—creating a family atmosphere filled with laughter, enjoyment and some of the sheer silliness of daily living. Sometimes we forget about the beneficial effects of laughter, how it strengthens the immune system, combats illness, and contributes an upbeat tone to the quality of our lives.

Children are very funny, and we adults are downright comical at times too. We can do our children and ourselves a great favor by promoting and indulging in laughter at home and by not taking ourselves so seriously. Kids think it's great fun when their parents laugh, especially when they are able to laugh at themselves.

UNREALISTIC EXPECTATIONS

As we make changes or try to do something new, we sometimes become discouraged when things do not run smoothly or positive results are not achieved immediately. We should know from experience that the real world doesn't work that way. This can be especially frustrating when we have made plans involving the whole family, and at the last minute one of the children refuses to participate, or a change in a family routine meets with strong resistance, or a child acts out in some way and a family conflict erupts. These are not times to lose heart.

Families—like groups, organizations, cities, and nations—start and stop, miss a few times, and then start over again. When the word *regular* is used in conjunction with a proposed activity or game plan, we must recognize that it simply won't happen every time. At times, the solution to one problem will create another.

We need to be committed to the notion that a philosophy, a strategy or a good idea is not to be abandoned simply because of obstacles or mistakes. These come with the territory and provide new opportunities for creative thinking.

Taking Control of Your Life

So what's a parent to do? How do you get everything done in the limited time available? The answer is to take control of your life. Recognize that some of the pressures you feel are self-imposed and unnecessary. Begin by recognizing these and getting rid of them. Remind yourself that no matter how much you have to do or how limited your resources are, there are always choices to be made and by making them, stress can be reduced. However, you must be ready to let go of being overwhelmed. Some parents are always overwhelmed; others are under-whelmed. The goal here is to get everyone just "whelmed."

Becoming a professional at parenting means becoming a more conscious parent. It means recognizing that if you feel overwhelmed, it's an indication that you are doing too much and/or behaving inefficiently. The following are suggestions to help you move toward taking better control of your life.

PREPARE PRELIMINARY TO-DO LIST

Carrying in your head the details of everything you have to or want to do is both a strain and inefficient. The first step in taking control of your life is to make a written list of everything you believe (or imagine) you have to do in the next 90 days. Brainstorm this list and do it quickly, without dwelling on any item. If glancing at your preliminary list indicates that there is more to do than time available—which is usually the case—rethink your situation and eliminate any item that you feel is not essential. If you want to do it eventually, place it on a "future" list.

PRIORITIZE AND SCHEDULE

At this stage, you need to make conscious decisions as to which activities/tasks are most important so that they don't get overlooked, neglected, or short-changed. Select things you feel must be done in the next 30 days.

Prepare a 30-day calendar allocating specific days and time blocks for each activity, using your knowledge of the family situation, your own behavior, and the activities involved.

This is your conscious thinking as to the most practical days and time of day to get things done efficiently.

By creating a written plan, you will frequently find there is not enough time to achieve everything you had in mind. In this case, you must either create additional time or postpone or eliminate something on the schedule.

CREATING ADDITIONAL TIME

Extend the Workday

Unfortunately, many parents try to gain time by going to sleep later and/or getting up earlier. This is not recommended. It's what leads to being overwhelmed. It's better to select one or more of the suggestions described below. In an urgent situation, a longer day is always an option.

Create More Time by Simplifying Various Aspects of Your Life

If you were to follow anyone around for an entire day, you would find a considerable amount of wasted or inefficient use of time—much more than most of us realize. This contributes significantly to our feelings of stress. A few examples are:

◆ Too many trips for errands which could be combined

◆ Procrastination

◆ Unnecessary phone calls and/or long phone calls

◆ Not preparing things for the next day

◆ Agreeing to do something which you really didn't want or need to do

◆ Not concentrating on one thing at a time, and accumulating a backlog of unfinished tasks

◆ Not setting priorities

◆ Allowing too many distractions, such as turning on the TV for a short break which then becomes a long one.

Do Some Things Less Thoroughly or Less Frequently

Not everything has to be done with the same thoroughness or frequency. You can have a family activity every other week rather than every week, do a major house cleaning once a month rather than weekly, shop for food only once a week, and so forth.

Delegate

Get help from your spouse, children, and extended family (grandparents, siblings, other relatives). Parenting is a full-time responsibility, but parents are not the only ones who can be caregivers and household helpers. Sharing household responsibilities with children has multiple benefits. In addition to lessening the pressure on parents, it provides an opportunity for children to acquire some skills and to feel important. Extended family can help with baby-sitting, tutoring, and much more.

Barter

Exchange help with someone (e.g., look after a neighbor's children along with your own and have them do the same for you).

Pay for help

Where economically feasible, pay someone to handle certain tasks to reduce workload and/or provide free time. Even where money is a problem, sacrificing something material for household or childcare help is a trade-off worth considering.

Networking

Create or join a support group where parents help one another with certain tasks on a rotating basis and support one another in many different ways.

Reduce Unnecessary Worry

Cut down on the amount of psychic energy that goes into unnecessary worrying about your child. Yes, the world is a dangerous place and there are many things to be concerned about. On the other hand, you can make yourself miserable 24 hours a day with unproductive and unrealistic worrying. It can help to reduce some of this worry by distinguishing between low- and high-risk activities, and by recognizing that because something is possible doesn't mean it's probable. Concentrate your efforts on the high-risk, high-probability areas. Minimize or eliminate concern in the low-risk, low-probability realm.

Reduce Negative Effects of False Emergencies, Interruptions, and Distractions

Some emergencies and interruptions cannot be avoided and must be handled without delay. Other ones are not real and should not require an immediate response and sometimes no response at all. Parents need to discern one from the other.

(For an abundance of additional timesaving ideas, Appendix A—*Guide to Parent Resources*—contains descriptions of two excellent books, Kathy Peel's *The Family Manager's Guide for Working Moms,* and Elaine St. James', *Simplify Your Life With Kids.*)

ONGOING PLANNING AND REVISION

Given the possibilities described above to parent smarter rather than harder, you are in a position to (a) prepare a plan that is more realistic, less stressful, and more productive, and (b) to evaluate results and make adjustments along the way. Evaluation of the schedule involves looking at what was actually done in relation to what was originally planned, and deciding what, if anything, could have been done better. The longer you stay with the process, the more skilled you become and the easier it gets.

Summing Up

There always will be conflicts between the things that you need to get done for your family, your career, and your own personal nurturing. You will never be able to do everything. Time is limited and tasks to be performed are unlimited, but you can only do what you can do. Having a framework for making conscious decisions about trade-offs, compromises and adjustments will ease the task, but it won't be easy. It will require discipline, practice, and perseverance, but it is worth the effort. After all, if it doesn't work, you can always go back to being overwhelmed!

A final thought—no matter how good you get at taking control of your life, there always will be moments of feeling overwhelmed. At these times, you might well consider the following advice suggested to me by a mother: "When all hell seems to be breaking loose, and I am feeling overwhelmed— there are dishes in the sink, dinner hasn't been prepared, shopping needs to be done, the house is a mess, the baby is crying, my back is hurting, and I feel like screaming—I've learned to stop, take a deep breath, and ask myself, 'What's the most important thing I can do right now?' Then I pick up my baby, sit down with her on my lap in the living room, take the phone off the hook and do nothing for a while. It's amazing how things seem to fall into place after that."

S I X

Strengthening
Families and Schools

(Creating and Extending
a Sense of Community)

Families

A SENSE OF COMMUNITY

Ideally, families would function as a team in the best tradition of the word, as in: *team effort*—everyone pulls together for the good of the whole; *team play*—collective play with mutual assistance of members; *teamwork*—several associates each doing a part, subordinating personal prominence to the efficiency of the whole. In practice, however, some families seem closer to another definition, *team*—two or more draft animals harnessed to the same vehicle.

John Gardner, former U.S. Secretary of Health, Education, and Welfare, once said, "The problem with many of our cities is that they are encampments of strangers and not communities." This is also a problem with many families. Too often in our modern, complex, fast-moving, high-tech societies, families do not always develop a sense of community, and children get lost in the rush. To create this sense of community, families need to be involved with one another—to do things together.

117

Families that do things together create camaraderie and co-hesion. Families that do things together that are fun and interesting create a positive atmosphere. Families that do things together that encourage members to think, ask questions, and express themselves become learning communities. Families that do things together on a regular basis create traditions. Families that create traditions develop a strong sense of community, displaying mutual respect, caring, and support. The children of families with a strong sense of community are more resistant to outside negative influences, more likely to be influenced by positive role models within the family and to become emotionally healthy citizens at home, in school, and within society at large.

Core Values

The strength of the family emanates from parents and their convictions. If there is no coherent philosophy, strategy, or approach to child rearing, and if values are not clear, parent behavior is usually inconsistent and confusing. It behooves parents to define values for themselves and to emphasize them in the family through words and action. If we think of family values as values shared by all members of the family, it becomes something very much worth striving for.

Adopting the five critical needs as an integral component of a family's core values provides a valuable framework to guide parents' interactions with their children and to evaluate their parenting effectiveness. Additionally, it does much more. As parents treat each other in ways that satisfy the five needs, they become role models for the kids on how to act in a loving way. Further, as parents communicate to children that they have the same needs and express positive feelings about the children's behavior that satisfy these needs, they begin to become true family values. Children are stimulated to start thinking not only about what's being done and not done to, for, and with them, but also about how their behavior impacts others.

Since the five needs are relevant to all interactions among individuals, opportunities to apply them in everyday life are constant. Thus, with practice, the children's and parents' understanding, appreciation, and use of the concepts are certain to grow. Children can learn about the power of their behavior to impact each other—and their parents—and also relatives, friends, teachers, and acquaintances—almost anyone with whom they have contact. This helps to strengthen a sense of community among family members, and it also gives children a larger view of community.

Self-Sacrifice/Self-Care/Balance

Most everyone would agree that parenting involves sacrifice and self-denial. However, there is a point where both can be overdone to the detriment of parent and child. If we become so obsessed with our responsibilities as parents that we are tense, exhausted, or irritable much of the time, we will be harming ourselves, our children, and probably our marriage. It is not necessary to be doing something for and with our children all the time; providing some *alone time* for kids to manage themselves—for their own amusement, interest, exploration, and discovery—can be a significant part of their growth. Often, what impacts children strongly about their childhood is whether the home was a pleasant, relaxed place—where mom and dad were fun to be around, rather than a family atmosphere filled with tension, worry, and confusion.

As important as it is to nurture our children, it is equally necessary to nurture ourselves—the two are closely related. Yes, parents need to sacrifice for their children, but this should not mean giving up all personal goals or desires. We need to learn how to sacrifice without sacrificing ourselves totally. For some, this might mean staying at home full time; for others it will involve a part- or full-time career. For all parents, it must include finding some guilt-free time for personal pursuits such as social contacts, travel, sports, exercise, reading, solitude, charity-work. It's healthy for parents and for children to have time by themselves.

Parents consciously need to seek as much balance as possible between career and home, work and play, time together and time alone in order to achieve an emotionally healthy family with a strong sense of community.

FIRST FIVE YEARS OF LIFE

Many new parents are so excited and filled with joy at the birth of their child that the complexity and enormity of parenting doesn't hit them right away. Soon, however, they begin to face the realities of 24 hours a day of constant responsibility and caring for the newborn.

In preparing for the act of giving birth, parents sometimes spend months during pregnancy in classes, discussion groups, and reading about the physical aspects of childbirth, and this time is well spent. Parents learn about some of the difficulties they will face and take steps to avoid them through diet, physical conditioning, and relaxation exercises. Preparation for meeting the child's critical emotional needs should also begin during pregnancy, and behavior to meet these emotional needs should begin at the same time and continue through infancy and thereafter.

Given the general agreement among experts as to the importance of the early years of life in the healthy development of children, getting them off to the best possible start should be primary in our thinking. Significantly, the Perinatal Services Network, under the auspices of the First 5 Commission, a California State program, purchased 60,000 copies of *How to Raise Emotionally Healthy Children*. They are being distributed to parents of newborn babies by childcare providers at 19 hospitals and incorporated into various parent-education programs.

The African-American Peer Counseling Project is one example of how an organization has integrated the concepts into the curriculum of a parent-education program. In each session of a five-part program, parents learn why and how to satisfy one of the five needs. As the program coordinator writes, "Because your book asks the readers to look into their own past and express how they felt as children, it opened up the floodgates for feelings that have never been addressed before. It has enabled the parents to open themselves to change. The women feel empowered by your book and are taking steps to make sure they are raising emotionally healthy children."

The Santa Barbara Graduate Institute, Department of Prenatal and Perinatal Psychology, has prepared an outline describing how each of the five needs can be satisfied by parents of infants. (See Appendix J—*Five Emotional Needs of Babies*.) Also, see Appendix J for information on obtaining important media resources regarding babies.

TEENAGERS

Adopting the five critical needs and a professional approach to parenting early in a child's life will go a long way to reducing problems parents experience when children become teenagers. However, even when this approach is started late, there are many benefits to be derived.

Teenagers can come to recognize that parents are not their adversaries—that every night just before they go to sleep, parents do not make up a list entitled, "How Many Ways Can I Make My Child Miserable Tomorrow." On the contrary, children can learn that parents have the same five critical needs as they do. And that sometimes, although parents generally try to act with a child's best interest in mind, they are not perfect and don't always make the right decision.

Understanding and accepting that parents are fallible, teenagers can learn that differences and conflicts can best be resolved through discussion, compromise and, yes, sometimes acceptance of parental authority. Children can learn that by assisting parents in meeting the parents' needs, they can get along better and get more of what they want. For example, understanding the parents' need to feel secure about their children's safety, they will recognize that it won't help, when borrowing the family car, to say, "I promise you I won't have an accident." That would not be reassuring, nor would it likely get the teenagers the permission they seek. Specifying the steps they intend to take to insure safety and soliciting suggestions from their parents would be much more effective.

Equally important is parents sharing more of their feelings and values directly with their children and making their desires known as to how they want to be treated. Parents have the responsibility for communicating their emotional needs so that teenagers can hear and understand them. Teenagers feel more secure when they observe that Mom and Dad are in accord regarding child rearing, and they are committed to treating each other and the kids in ways that satisfy the five critical needs.

For all children, not just teenagers, growing up in a family where meeting everyone's needs is emphasized, one of the goals and anticipated outcomes will be movement away from self-centeredness. Children will learn the importance and value of interacting with their parents, siblings, and others in ways that contribute to satisfying everyone's emotional needs. Further, this philosophy and attitude will be carried into adulthood so that when they become parents, their children will reap the benefits.

GRANDPARENTS

Grandparents can make an important contribution to the richness of family life as active extended-family members. The grandchildren can be the recipients of affection, gifts, family history, storytelling, tutoring, advice, vacation trips, family celebrations, and perspectives on various stages of life. Parents benefit from grandparents providing support such as encouragement and advice, help with the kids, and financial support for various necessities and luxuries.

However, as in all relations, problems arise. For example, grandparents visiting their children and grandchildren may criticize how their grandchildren are being raised—that is, lack of discipline, dirty room, impolite, spoiled, speak too much or too little—these critiques often delivered without tact or good timing. Also, when the grandparents babysit they sometimes do things contrary to the parents' explicit instructions such as not getting the kids to bed on time, giving them too many sweets, letting them watch prohibited TV programs, and more. This is not earth-shattering, and many parents adjust to it without difficulty. Sometimes their rationale is that grandparents don't spend much time with children anyway, so it's okay if they spoil them a little. For other parents though, it causes different degrees of stress and frustration, leading to strained relations, including diminished communication, socializing, or support.

Those who don't like the feeling of "walking on eggs" during visits may want to consider ways to improve the relationship. For example, they can begin a process of learning to confront differences in a way that might prove to be constructive. As a first step, I suggest that parents and grandparents read *How to Raise Emotionally Healthy Children* and discuss the concepts. The next step would be to establish an adult family-feedback session to meet once or twice monthly, in a comfortable setting, for an hour or two, without interruption.

The purpose would be to share feelings and thoughts in answer to the question, "What do we see each other, or ourselves, doing that is getting in the way or helping us to create a healthy, happy environment for the children and us?" (The process is described in Chapter 4, *Game Plan #3*.) The following are a few guidelines for having productive meetings:

- As parents and grandparents, you have the same five needs as the children, so interact with each other in ways that honor these; when this is done, the probability of positive outcomes is increased.

- To avoid adversarial relations, remember the purpose is not to prove a point, win an argument, or establish blame, but rather to develop mutual understanding as to the source of friction and possible solutions.

- Adopt the attitude that the grandparents mean well— that is, their criticism is an attempt to point to something that in their view is not good for the children.

- Accept the grandparents' right to their opinion, even though you may disagree with it strongly; therefore don't dismiss it, ignore, or trivialize it. Show that you have heard it, and then present your point of view— engage in the give and take in this way. Do more active listening than speaking, or at least as much.

- At the conclusion of a session, express appreciation for having received frank feedback and, where possible, indicate what outcomes might occur.

Remember, the test of character for a family or any relationship is not the absence of stress, friction, or conflicts, but rather how they are handled. Also, parents, don't forget that you will probably be grandparents some day; this can be good training for your future role.

SINGLE-PARENT FAMILIES

Much of what we have described in this book applies equally to single-parent families. In many ways, it is even more important for the single parent to have the core philosophy of the five critical needs as a foundation for parenting. Having more responsibility and less time to spend with the kids puts a premium on maximizing the time together—the five needs would provide a structure for more positive and consistent interactions. Also, despite the pressures and limitations of time, the single parent must not overlook what was stated in the section on self-nurturing and seeking a balanced lifestyle. Admittedly more difficult, it is still possible and necessary for the single parent to create time for socializing and time alone. Networking with other parents (e.g., joining a parent support group as described in Chapter 4, *Game Plan #12*) is one way that would be worthwhile.

PARENTS IN SECOND MARRIAGES

With the high divorce rate and subsequent large numbers of remarriages, step-parenting becomes an important consideration. Many stepparents and stepchildren find the situation uncomfortable and difficult. Living with someone else's children can be awkward and frustrating, adding to the normal stresses of a second marriage. Here, the structure of game plans, as described in Chapter 4, can offer the stepparents a more comfortable and effective way to create positive relations with their spouse's children. Traditional methods of imposing parental authority can be counterproductive. Positive parent-child relations will require patience, emphasis on satisfying the children's emotional needs and not overreacting to occasional negative behavior. Remember, this is a transitional, learning period. Family activities discussed in Chapter 1, under *Inclusion* and *Security,* can be useful in learning about one another. After you have read the book, having your teenagers and pre-teens read it and then discuss it with you, can be advantageous, but it is not something that should be forced.

SUMMING UP

Currently, there is much talk in society about the breakup of the family—the lack of cohesiveness, closeness, and family values. There are obviously strong elements influencing family members that pull them in different directions. You will need to have a clear vision of what you want your family life to be like and a committed approach to achieving it. In essence, it requires focus, time, and effort. Wishful thinking and desire alone will not help. Thinking about it and planning will.

If we think about the family as a community—a learning community—it gives us a different perspective; it's not just parents raising children but also children raising parents, all learning from one another; it means learning how to work and how to play, how to laugh and how to cry, how to be together and be by oneself, how to listen and how to speak, and how to love and be loved. These are things you don't learn just from books or from good teachers, although they will help; they are learned by becoming engaged in community and recognizing that community is not a spectator sport. It means being involved with one another, sometimes in struggle and pain but also in interesting, uplifting, and pleasurable endeavors, with fun and laughter as high priorities.

Making conscious decisions, having a plan, being students of our own behavior, and having an experimental attitude will increase the probability of becoming the kind of family we would like to be.

Adopting the five critical emotional needs as a family value would be an important factor in creating an emotionally healthy context in which to pursue all goals.

Family as a Learning Comunity

As parents and children become better students of their own behavior, they are able to help one another recognize when they are relating in emotionally healthy or unhealthy ways. This is the beginning of the family as a *learning community.* As such, it is no longer business as usual, with parents as paragons of knowledge and virtue to be passed on to their kids so they can become just like their moms and dads. It recognizes that adults are not finished products but rather *adults in training—* imperfect, fallible human beings. Family members understand that *all of them* need to learn how to become better persons, and that this learning can occur as a family—children from parents, parents from children, and all together. As part of this process, parents should consider having their teenagers (and where appropriate pre-teens too) read this book and discuss it together as a family—chapter by chapter, situation by situation, and game plan by game plan. Such a discussion, with its accompanying personal sharing, could further their getting to know one another better as people and not just in the roles of mother, father, and child.

Schools

Next to the family, the schools have perhaps the greatest influence in meeting the five critical needs of children. Unfortunately, the schools are plagued by as many difficulties as the beleaguered families. The problems of low achievement, inadequate financing, declining student and teacher morale, and poor school/parent relations persist from one decade to the next, and the dissatisfaction voiced by almost everyone is accompanied by increasingly stronger demands for change.

The need for cost-effective educational models that offer constructive, positive changes that are fundamental and systemic rather than superficial or limited has never been greater. Because of the diversity of schools and the constant pressure on students, parents, teachers, and administrators, models are needed that cut across geographical, ethnic, and socioeconomic boundaries. These models need to create a cooperative, friendly relationship among all the principal stakeholders and a sense of ownership in our schools. *The Children's Project* was designed for this purpose.

THE CHILDREN'S PROJECT AND
THE FIVE CRITICAL NEEDS

In spite of all the discussion about change, there has been hardly a whisper about the failure to meet the emotional needs of our children; yet this continues to be one of the most serious problems jeopardizing the future of our children and our nation. To make matters worse, the educational community and policymakers appear to be oblivious to the problem. A major purpose of *The Children's Project* is to fill this troublesome void.

The Children's Project is a grass-roots, non-commercial effort, initiated by Deborah Newmark, Executive Director, and myself, and based on this book, *How to Raise Emotionally Healthy Children*. It is a model for our "emotional-health-friendly school" concept, which is applicable to every level of education and inclusive of all types of schools, programs, and populations. Its influence can be far reaching, because the concept of the five critical emotional needs is fundamental and contributes to success in school, work, marriage, and life in general.

VISION

Our vision is one of a school where parents and teachers work individually and together to meet the emotional needs of children at home and at school—where adults interact with children, and with one another, in emotionally healthy ways. The book provides a common language—that of the five critical emotional needs—to bring home and school, parent and teacher closer together—reinforcing one another's efforts to provide children an emotional foundation for success.

Just imagine what an impact this could have on the children's emotional, intellectual, and social learning if all the teachers in the same school (pre-school through high school), year after year, were meeting the same emotional needs of children that the parents were satisfying at home.

As children experience throughout their school life what it's like to feel *respected, important, accepted, included,* and *secure* (the opposite of what most children now experience), and these needs become a home and school value, the kids are more likely to become self-confident, independent, thinking, caring, civic-minded individuals.

TEACHING/LEARNING PROGRAM

The following are the basic elements of the teaching/learning program recommended for using the book in schools.

Each parent and teacher receives a free copy of *How to Raise Emotionally Healthy Children* from the sponsoring school. They are encouraged to engage in the following activities.

Parents

(1) **Learn by Doing**—Read the book and immediately begin to implement the concepts in the daily interactions with their children.

(2) **Conscious Parenting**—Keeping a Daily Journal/Becoming A Student of Your Own Behavior

At the end of each day, they take about 15 minutes to complete a brief questionnaire about their contribution to satisfying any of the children's five critical needs and what they learned about their own behavior. These learnings are a guide for future interactions.

(3) **Mutual Support**—Parent Support Group

Parents meet for six weekly sessions in a small group to share information, ask questions, present problems, give and receive feedback, and exchange ideas—those who wish can continue in successive sessions throughout the year. Sometimes a trained counselor or a facilitator guides the group, other times it may be a teacher, a non-professional leader or a leaderless group.

Teachers

Adapt *Learning by Doing* and *Conscious Parenting* concepts for their classrooms; recommend to parents to participate in support groups; conduct occasional parent orientations; confer with individual parents as necessary.

High School and College Students

Seminars on Parent/Child Relations are provided to the students. Students listen to and discuss brief lectures, participate in interactive exercises, read the book, write book reports, and discuss the material. Students have been positive about the value of the material when they get married and have their own children—also in present relations with their parents, fellow students, friends, and significant others.

SUMMING UP

Parents who read this book to improve their parenting effectiveness invariably recognize the significance for their own relationship. That is, they see the value of treating each other with the five needs in mind. Thus, the children benefit not only from being treated in emotionally healthy ways but also in observing how their parents treat each other.

Students arriving at school will be better prepared to learn and to interact with others. This facilitates the teacher's task. If the teacher adopts the five needs as a classroom value, the children's development will be more rapid and deeper, especially if this continues in all classes until the students graduate. This, of course, makes the parents' job at home much easier too. As parent-student-teacher relationships become closer, it's a win-win for all concerned. (For a view of a high school vision that does justice to the five critical needs—to be *respected, important, accepted, included,* and *secure*—see Appendix K, *Role of Secondary Education in a Democratic and Changing Society.*)

Concluding Thoughts

As we approach the future, it is evident that technological progress has far outdistanced progress in human relations. In spite of miracles in technology, science, and medicine, when it comes to human relations, it seems at times that we are still living in the Dark Ages. We find conflict at every level of society—family, neighborhood, city, country, worldwide. It is a "luxury" we can no longer afford—we never could.

But where do we start? As individuals, we frequently feel overwhelmed in thinking about our national and world problems. Nevertheless, we can and must contribute by focusing on where we are able to have the most immediate impact—with ourselves, our children, our families, our schools, our neighborhoods, and communities.

As we focus on our own children, let us begin by strengthening the bonds between the parents themselves. Simultaneously, we need to extend our love to our children by treating them in the same way. Further, let's involve ourselves in our schools and help them develop the same sense of community we strive for in our families.

Also, we need to extend ourselves outward. We may not have a large extended family, but we can extend our family by loving all children. We need to do this not only because of our humanity, but also because it is in our enlightened self-interest to do so. With millions of children considered "at risk" in our society, all of us are at risk; as long as this situation continues to exist, no matter how well off we may be, there is no way to protect our children or ourselves from the crime, violence, and chaos that exist in too many of our schools, neighborhoods, and cities.

So, yes, we must love not only our own kids but all kids—that includes the kids across the street, on the next block, and on the other side of town, and in other countries. But what does it mean to love all children? Does it have any practical implications? It does not mean that every time we see a kid, we stop him and say, "Hi kid, I love you." It does mean that we treat all kids in a loving way.

It means that every contact with any child, even a casual contact, is an opportunity to act with courtesy and respect, and to not talk down in a patronizing way. It means when you meet a parent and child at a supermarket and greet the parent, you say "hello" to the child, too. When children are in our presence at a dinner or other social gatherings with friends and relatives, we shouldn't ignore them; we should show some interest and include them in some of our conversation without pressuring them to perform in front of others against their will.

We might go further by becoming a mentor, paying for a kid's summer camp trip, or deciding to provide ongoing support for a child—perhaps an at-risk child. We might decide to adopt a child or become a foster parent. At another level, we may join efforts to fight hunger, child abuse, drugs, or participate in other children's causes. Once it becomes part of our psyche that we are our brother's keeper—that all children are our children—we will find ways to make more of them a significant part of our thoughts and lives.

Families and schools must join in a partnership to make children our number-one priority and, guided by an ethos of love and pragmatism, move vigorously and with determination from talk to action. By creating a positive atmosphere in which people interact with people in ways that make everyone feel *respected, important, accepted, included,* and *secure,* we can become a powerful force for developing emotionally healthy and high-achieving children, families, and schools— our own and those of others. And, who knows? If enough of us get involved, we might just change the world.

Epilogue

The Great Dictator (1940) *by* Charlie Chaplin

(Excerpt from farewell speech of the accidental dictator
at the end of the film.)

I'm sorry, but I don't want to be an emperor. I don't want to rule or conquer anyone.

I should like to help everyone, if possible—Jew, Gentile, black men, white . . .

We all want to help one another. Human beings are like that.

We want to live by each other's happiness, not by each other's misery . . .

The way of life can be beautiful, but we have lost the way.

Greed has poisoned men's souls, has barricaded the world with hate, has goose-stepped us into misery and bloodshed.

We have developed speed, but we have shut ourselves in.

Machinery that gives abundance has left us in want.

Our knowledge has made us cynical; our cleverness hard and unkind.

We think too much and feel too little.

More than machinery we need humanity.

More than cleverness, we need kindness and gentleness.

Without these qualities, life will be violent, and all will be lost.

Guide to Parent Resources
(Tools for Life-Long Learning)

Of the many excellent publications available on parenting, we have selected a limited number that represent sound theory and are action-oriented. These books include valuable information and a large variety of activities and projects for children to do on their own, with others, or with the entire family. They span all age levels and contribute to satisfying one or more of a child's five critical emotional needs. Most of these books are available in paperback and can be found in libraries, bookstores, or through Amazon.com (including low-cost and out-of-print books).

Resources for Learning

Ames, Louise Bates and Ilg, Frances L. (Series on child growth and development with other collaborators: Haber, Carol Chase, and Baker, Sidney M.)

Drs. Ames and Ilg are recognized worldwide authorities on child behavior and development. Under the auspices of the Gesell Institute of Human Behavior, which they co-founded in 1950, they have authored an authoritative series of 10 volumes on child behavior and development. The first nine books cover ages 1 to 9 (each book one year), and the tenth deals with ages 10 to 14. These books describe the physical, emotional, and psychological development of children in an informative and interesting manner, offering much practical and expert advice about dealing with child behavior. This series is an outstanding resource for helping parents better understand their children at different stages of life.

Benson, L., Galbraith, J., Espeland, P. *What Kids Need to Succeed.* Minneapolis: Free Spirit Publishing, 1995. (167 pp.)

Based on a nationwide study, this book describes 30 assets— good things young people need—and over 500 concrete suggestions to build these assets at home, at school, and in the community. These represent a large variety of specific activities that can be done alone, with family, and with others that will contribute to a child's sense of accomplishment, self-esteem, and service.

Bell, R., and Wildflower, L.Z. *Talking With Your Teenager.* New York: Random House, 1983. (127 pp.)

The authors emphasize that good communication between parents and teenagers can be facilitated by parents' awareness of what their children are experiencing during adolescence. This book gives detailed information about puberty, emotional health, sexuality, drug/alcohol use, and eating disorders, so that parents can discuss these issues with their children knowledgeably and compassionately. They share with readers suggestions from a large number of parents for improving parent-teenager interactions.

Brazelton, T. Berry. *Touchpoints: Your Child's Emotional and Behavioral Development.* Reading, Mass.: Perseus Books, 1992. (479 pp.)

Dr. Brazelton is recognized internationally as perhaps the most authoritative expert in the field of child development. His years of experience as a practicing pediatrician, researcher, and teacher uniquely qualify him to provide parents with an understanding of child development from a physical, cognitive, emotional, and behavioral point of view. *Touchpoints* contains a wealth of information that helps parents deal effectively with childrearing problems, while reducing parents' anxiety and stress and enabling them to prevent future problems.

Curran, Dolores. *Traits of a Healthy Family*. New York: Ballantine Books, 1983. (315 pp.)

The author surveyed 500 professionals—teachers, doctors, pastors, Boy Scout and Girl Scout leaders, social workers, and others—to come up with 15 traits most often found in healthy families. Rather than looking at problems, this book focuses on the strength of families. As such, it provides a valuable resource for evaluating the strengths of one's family and is a source of ideas and actions for making it stronger.

Davis, L., and Keyser, J. *Becoming the Parent You Want to Be: A Sourcebook of Strategies for the First Five Years*. New York: Broadway Books, 1997. (426 pp.)

This is a comprehensive book covering the first five years of childhood. To facilitate the task of lifelong learning, the authors present nine principles to guide the parenting journey. It is a family-friendly resource that provides much developmental information to help parents understand children's behavior. It offers a wealth of concrete answers to immediate questions related to food, sleep, discipline, conflict, tantrums, and hundreds of other concerns that arise. It also helps parents define their own goals and how to use their creativity for problem solving.

Gordon, Thomas. *P.E.T. Parent Effectiveness Training: The Tested Way to Raise Responsible Children*. New York: Plume, 1975. (329 pp.)

First published in 1970, this is one of the most widely read and readable books on parent training. With its clear language, emphasis on specific skills, and usable methods, it continues to provide parents with practical help in dealing with problems of child rearing and also in preventing them. Parents have learned that they can use the book to develop skills on their

own, without necessarily taking P.E.T. classes. Most of the excellent material gives parents additional tools to use in meeting the five critical needs of children.

Lazear, J. and Lazear, W. L. *Meditations for Parents Who Do Too
Much*. New York: Simon & Schuster, 1993. (365 pp.)

This is a small, stimulating book of 365 brief meditations
related to the innumerable concerns most parents have or have
had at one time or another. It includes much good advice for
parents on how to reduce stress in themselves and their children. Although it takes only two or three minutes to read each
meditation, you'll find many nuggets of wisdom. It emphasizes slowing down and enjoying parenting more.

Lewis, B. A. *The Kid's Guide to Service Projects: Over 500 Service
Ideas for Young People Who Want to Make a Difference*. Minneapolis: Free Spirit Publishing, 1995. (175 pp.)

This is an excellent resource for civic-minded families. Contains over 500 service ideas in areas such as community development, crime fighting, environment, friendship, health,
holidays, homelessness, hunger, literacy, people with special
needs, politics and government, safety, senior citizens, and
transportation. The book also includes a discussion of ten
steps for creating successful projects.

Lofas, Jeannette, with Sova, Dawn B. *Stepparenting: Everything
You Need to Know to Make It Work!* New York: Kensington
Books, 1996 (228 pp.)

The subtitle tells it all. Anyone who is in a relationship or a
marriage that involves children from a previous marriage will
find a wealth of information about all aspects of stepparenting. Many issues are discussed that act as barriers to a healthy
adult-child relationship, starting with parents' initial dating,
through establishing a common household and getting married. Many techniques are suggested for solving and preventing problems.

Madaras, L. *Talks to Teens About AIDS: An Essential Guide for Parents, Teachers, and Young People.* New York: Newmarket Press, 1988. (106 pp.)

AIDS is a frightening disease. The thought of it evokes much anxiety and fear among parents and inhibits their ability to discuss it adequately with their children. This book can serve parents, teachers, and teenagers as a tool for understanding and preventing the transmission of this disease. It separates facts from rumors—who gets it, what the symptoms are, how it is and isn't transmitted, and how to prevent it. The book is written in a direct, frank, and clear manner and will help parents and teenagers discuss AIDS effectively.

Marlor Press. *Kids Vacation Diary.* Saint Paul: Marlor Press, 1995. (95 pp.)

This is a workbook full of games and activities related to taking a trip, for children from 6-12 years old. These activities take place in three phases: getting ready for the trip, during the trip, and memories from the trip. In addition to being fun, the book presents opportunities for improving reading, writing, planning, decision making, and speaking skills. Although written with a vacation trip in mind, the diary can be adapted for home use.

Newmark, Gerald. *This School Belongs to You and Me: Every Learner a Teacher, Every Teacher a Learner.* New York: Hart Publishing Company, 1976. (431 pp.)

This book is a model of innovative education, describing a learning environment from kindergarten through 6th grade where the principal participants—children, parents, teachers, and administrators—share responsibility, authority, and accountability in revitalizing the educational process. Four major concepts govern the school; that is, shared learning/teaching (all students become teachers of each other as a central instructional method), shared planning, and decision making, shared feedback, and parent/community involvement. (Available through NMI Publishers, Tarzana, CA 91356)

Peel, Kathy. *The Family Manager's Guide for Working Moms.* New York: Ballantine Books, 1997. (202 pp.)

This is an excellent book for parents who want to learn more about organizing their time for maximum efficiency. It shows how to take skills from the business world and transfer them effectively to the home. Lots of ideas, techniques, methods, and strategies are presented for working smarter rather than harder. It is not only for working mothers but also for any busy parent who feels under stress. Adopting even a few of the ideas will yield immediate benefits and lighten the load.

St. James, Elaine. *Simplify Your Life With Kids: 100 Ways to Make Life Easier and More Fun.* Kansas City, MO: Andrews McNeel Publishing, 1997. (361 pp.)

A rich source of ideas for simplifying your life with kids, written in an interesting conversational style. Provides practical, down-to-earth advice on almost every aspect of your life with kids from the time they awaken in the morning until they are fast asleep at night and everything in between. Covers areas such as daily routines, workload, accumulation of "stuff," telephone management, getting help, family teamwork, simplifying handling of discipline and conflict, simple celebrations, family issues, school and after school, travel, health and much more—all from the point of view of making things easier.

Spock, B. M., M.D. *A Better World for Our Children: Rebuilding American Family Values.* Betheseda, MD: National Press Books, 1994. (205 pp.)

This is a book by the dean of child-rearing experts. It empowers parents to influence the future of their children and provides specific activities that families can do together to make a difference in their homes and neighborhoods. These activities contribute to family solidarity and to the young person's self-esteem and have many positive by-products.

Stock, G. *The Kids Book of Questions.* New York: Workman Publishing, 1988. (207 pp.)

Two hundred sixty interesting, thought-provoking questions—including a few playful ones. The questions deal with serious issues and dilemmas that children and adults face throughout life (e.g., dealing with authority, understanding friendship, handling social pressures, overcoming fears, making ethical choices, and much more). It can serve as a valuable weekly or monthly family activity in which each member answers a question, followed by discussion.

York, P. and York, D. *Toughlove: A Self-Help Manual for Parents Troubled by Teenage Behavior.* Sellersville, PA: Community Service Foundation, 1980.

This is a manual for parents of teenagers who have serious, ongoing problems such as truancy, running away from home, alcohol/drug abuse, and/or trouble with the law. These are the teenagers sometimes considered incorrigible, who have not responded to guidance counselors, caring parents, or authority. It is for parents for whom nothing has worked. The manual explains what "Toughlove" is, who needs it, and spells out a blueprint for putting it into action.

Group for Environmental Education, Inc. *Yellow Pages of Learning Resources.* Philadelphia, 1972.

This is a book concerned with the potential of the city as a place for learning. It calls our urban environments "classrooms without walls," which offer people of all ages endless opportunities. It emphasizes that all the people, places, and events of the community at-large represent potentially rich resources for learning, which can and should be systematically exploited by our schools. It can also serve as a resource for parents working with their own kids.

Family Activities List

Check each item that might be of interest to you. Place a question mark next to any item about which you would like to know more. (Duplicate form and start your own notebook.)

Games

___ 20 Questions

___ Board Games (chess, checkers, monopoly, etc.)

___ Cards

___ Charades

___ Crossword Puzzles

___ Darts

___ Dice

___ Horseshoes

___ Jigsaw Puzzles

___ Table Games (pool, billiards)

Sports

___ Archery

___ Badminton

___ Ballooning

___ Baseball

___ Basketball

___ Bicycling

___ Bowling

___ Car Racing/Rallying

___ Croquet

___ Fencing

___ Football

___ Golf

___ Horseback Riding

___ Jogging

___ Judo

___ Kayaking

___ Lawn Bowling

___ Racquet Ball

___ Rowing

___ Sailing

___ Shooting

___ Skating

___ Skateboarding

___ Skiing (Snow, Water)

___ Snorkeling

___ Soccer

___ Sports Viewing

___ Squash

___ Swimming

___ Table Tennis

___ Tennis

___ Volleyball

___ Walking

Nature Activities

___ Animal Care

___ Astronomy

___ Barn Viewing

___ Beachcombing

___ Big Game Hunting

___ Bird Watching

___ Botany

___ Camping

___ Ecology/Conservation

___ Geology

___ Greenhouse Gardening

___ Hiking

___ Indoor Plant Raising

___ Meteorology

___ Mountain Climbing

___ Outdoor Gardening

___ Rock and Fossil Hunting

___ Trapping

___ Tropical Fish Breeding

___ Wild Food Gathering

___ Wildlife Observation

Collecting Activities

___ Antique (Books, Bottles, Dolls, etc.)

___ Buttons

___ Coins

___ Folk Art

___ Fossils

___ Models

___ Photographs (e.g., Airports, City Halls, Amusing Signs)

___ Postcards

___ Posters

___ Recipes

___ Rocks

___ Stamps

Crafts

___ Appliance Repair

___ Automobile Repair

___ Bookbinding

___ Candlemaking

___ Cooking and Baking

___ Decoupage

___ Floral Arranging

___ Furniture

___ Gourmet Cooking

___ House Decorating

___ Kit Assembling

___ Knitting

___ Leather

___ Miniatures

___ Origami

___ Quilting

___ Reupholstery

___ Rugs

___ Sausage Making

___ Scrapbooks

___ Sewing

___ Soldering and Welding

___ Toy Repairing

___ Whittling

___ Wine Making

Art and Music

___ Cartooning

___ Drawing

___ Film Production

___ Group Singing

___ Instrument Playing

___ Joke Telling

___ Lettering

___ Painting

___ Photography

___ Play Acting

___ Play Reading

___ Popular Dancing

___ Puppet Shows

___ Square Dancing

___ Ventriloquism

___ Wood Sculpture

Writing

___ Diary Keeping

___ Fiction Stories

___ Greeting Cards

___ Historical Stories

___ Letter Writing

___ Plays

___ Poetry

___ Short Stories

Social Activities

___ Group Listening

___ Discussion Groups

___ Home Entertaining

___ Visiting Friends

___ Dining Out

___ Picnics

___ Churchgoing

Education, Entertainment, and Cultural Activities

___ Genealogy

___ General Interest College Courses

___ Learning a Foreign Language

___ Reading—General

___ Reading—Special Projects

___ Listening to Classical Music

___ Listening to Popular Music

___ Theater Going

___ Movie Going

___ TV Watching, Analysis, and Evaluation

___ Attending Art Festivals

___ Attending Concerts

___ Visiting Museums

___ Visiting Zoos

___ Special Purpose Field Trips

___ Traveling

___ Going to Auctions

___ Going to Garage Sales and Flea Markets

___ TV Educational Courses

___ Figure and Weight Control

___ Individual Contemplation or Meditation

___ Yoga

___ Exercises

___ Skill Improvement Courses

Volunteer Activities

___ Blind Care

___ Boards of Directors

___ Building Maintenance

___ Children and Youth Group Services

___ Elderly Group Services

___ Foster Home Management

___ Fundraising

___ Library Aides

___ Museum Aides

___ Professional and Managerial Assistance

___ Reading for the Blind

___ Sheltered Workshop Instruction

___ Secretary/Bookkeeping Aides

___ Truck and Car Driving

Organizational Activities

___ Book Clubs

___ Collecting Clubs

___ Communication Clubs

___ Ethnic Organizations

___ Fraternal Organizations

___ Game Clubs

___ Hobby Groups

___ Intercultural Organizations

___ International Aid Groups

___ Nonpartisan Political and Social Action Groups

___ Outdoor Groups

___ Political Groups

___ Religious Groups

___ Service Clubs

___ Sports Clubs

Others

___

___

___

Becoming a Student of My Own Behavior

Date: _____ Child:_____

Keeping A Daily Journal

At the end of the day, take 15-20 minutes to briefly answer each of the questions below. (Duplicate form and start your own notebook.)

1. Which of my actions today were positive in regard to any of my child's five needs?

2. Which of my actions today were negative in regard to my child's five needs?

3. What did I learn about myself: attitudes, behavior, strengths, weaknesses?

4. If I were doing today over again, what would I do differently?

5. Comments and/or questions about my child's or my own attitudes and behavior. (For possible future discussion with spouse, parent support group, or parenting class)

146

Family Feedback Critique

Date of meeting:_____Length of time: _____

After the weekly feedback session, *briefly* answer the questions be-low. (Duplicate form and start your own notebook.)

1. What did I <u>like</u> about the meeting—in general—and about my participation?

2. What did I <u>dislike</u> about the meeting—in general—and about my participation?

3. What we might do differently at the next session is:

4. Questions and/or comments I have about the meeting are:

Parent Self-Care Plan

Date of meeting: _____ Length of time: _____
(Make a plan for 3, 6, or 12 months)

Complete questions #1 and #2 below, and then prepare a personal self-care plan. (Duplicate form and start your own notebook.)

1. List of activities I participate in and plan to continue for pleasure, leisure, health, and learning.

   <u>Activity</u>   <u>Frequency</u>   <u>With whom</u>

2. List of new activities I desire to add to, or in place of, any of the above.

   <u>Activity</u>   <u>Frequency</u>   <u>With whom</u>

3. Use the information in #1 and #2 above to prepare a 3, 6, or 12-month plan on a separate sheet. Be specific about activity, frequency, location, time, and with whom.

Parent Self-Care Evaluation

Date of meeting: _____ Length of time: _____
(Make a plan for 3, 6, or 12 months)

At the end of each month following the starting date of the plan, complete questions #1 and #2 below, and then prepare and review the plan after the following month if necessary. (Duplicate form and start your own notebook.)

1. To what extent was the plan implemented?

2. How satisfied am I with the results?

3. What helped or hindered implementation of the plan?

4. What did I learn about myself in regard to self-care: attitudes, behavior, strengths, weaknesses?

5. What changes are needed for the following month, either in the plan or in my behavior?

6. Comments and/or questions. (For future self-review discussion with spouse, parent support group, or parenting class)

Family Activities Plan

Date of meeting:_____ Length of time: _____
(If desired, plan for 3, 6, or 12 months)

Complete questions #1 and #2 below, and prepare a 3, 6, or 12-month family activities plan. (Duplicate form and start your own notebook.)

1. List below the activities the family participates in together.

    Activity   Frequency   Where   With whom

2. List of new activities we desire to add to, or in place of, any of above.

    Activity   Frequency   Where   With whom

3. Review #1 and #2 above, and prepare a 3, 6, or 12-month family plan on a separate form.

Family Activities Evaluation

Date:_____ Period: From _____ To_____

At the end of each month, *briefly* answer the following questions to assess (1) progress in implementing plan, (2) satisfaction with results, and (3) the need to make changes in plan or own behavior. (Duplicate form and start your own notebook.)

1. To what extent was the plan implemented?

2. What helped or hindered successful implementation of the plan?

3. What did you learn about yourself in regard to family activities: attitudes, behavior, strengths, weaknesses?

4. What changes are needed for the following month, either in the plan or in your behavior?

5. Comments and/or questions.

Children's Well-Being Survey

Complete periodically for each child, discuss with spouse, and decide on need for action or information. (Duplicate form and start your own notebook.)

Child _____ Date _____

	Not Well (Negative)			Well (Positive)			Not Sure
1. Health	1	2	3	4	5	6	X
a. Sleeping	1	2	3	4	5	6	X
b. Eating	1	2	3	4	5	6	X
c. Exercise	1	2	3	4	5	6	X
d. Energy	1	2	3	4	5	6	X
e. Illness	1	2	3	4	5	6	X
2. Attitudes/Behavior	1	2	3	4	5	6	X
a. Attitude toward life	1	2	3	4	5	6	X
b. Attitude toward people	1	2	3	4	5	6	X
c. Attitude toward family life	1	2	3	4	5	6	X
d. Self-respect	1	2	3	4	5	6	X
e. Respect for others	1	2	3	4	5	6	X
f. Self-confidence	1	2	3	4	5	6	X
g. Trust in others	1	2	3	4	5	6	X
h. Feels valued	1	2	3	4	5	6	X
i. Shows gratitude	1	2	3	4	5	6	X
j. Feels included	1	2	3	4	5	6	X
k. Includes others	1	2	3	4	5	6	X
l. Helpfulness	1	2	3	4	5	6	X
3. Leisure/Recreation Activities	1	2	3	4	5	6	X
4. Relationships	1	2	3	4	5	6	X
a. Parents	1	2	3	4	5	6	X
b. Brothers/Sisters	1	2	3	4	5	6	X
c. Other family members	1	2	3	4	5	6	X
d. Friends	1	2	3	4	5	6	X
e. Boy/Girl	1	2	3	4	5	6	X
5. Learning/School	1	2	3	4	5	6	X
6. Use of Time	1	2	3	4	5	6	X

Five Emotional Needs of Babies

1. Respect

- ♥ Acknowledge and talk to baby about what is going on around him or her
  - ○ Internal Environment
    - ■ Emotions – "You seem really mad that you can't have the . . . "
    - ■ Bodily functions (hunger, elimination) – "I'm going to change your diaper now."
    - ■ Awareness – "Are you smiling because you saw mommy smiling?"
    - ■ Sensations – "That was cold."
  - ○ External Environment
    - ■ Physical interactions with environment
    - ■ Communication
      - • Responding to baby's requests, needs
      - • Explaining why, what, who, when
      - • Acknowledge why not honoring baby's communication (why mother is not going to let baby down on a dirty bathroom floor)
- ♥ Look baby in the eyes – gazing
- ♥ Acknowledge and apologize to baby when caregiver fails to meet needs, wants of baby

2. Important

- ♥ Acknowledging and narrating baby's internal and external environment

♥ Going at baby's pace (slow)

♥ Showing baby caregiver's pleasure at seeing baby, especially upon reacquaintance after sleep or work

♥ Lots of eye contact

♥ Reading baby's cues (gestures, sounds, posture, emotions) about needs (contact, separateness, hunger, sleep, cleanliness, play/explore)

3. Accepted

♥ Caregiver is okay, calm with baby's intense emotional expressions (mad, scared, sad, happy)

♥ Caregiver can mirror baby's facial expressions and positive emotions

♥ Let baby know how wanted baby is (express gratitude for baby)

♥ Let baby know caregiver will always love and be there for baby – even if baby expresses negative emotions

4. Included

♥ Hold baby, sleep with baby, wear baby – take baby with caregiver, use a sling/carrier

♥ Ask baby permission, respond to answer respectfully and with acknowledgement

♥ Talk to baby, tone of voice (soft, higher pitched, melodic)

♥ Tell baby what is happening to baby (during bath, diapering, doctor's visit, play/exploring)

5. Secure

♥ Touch baby lovingly and often

♥ Be with baby as much as possible – hold baby, sleep with baby, wear baby (sling)

♥ Baby can express intense emotions (mad, scared, sad, happy), and caregiver can stay calm and not get stressed out

♥ Move slowly in interactions with and around baby

♥ Pick baby up within 90 seconds of when crying begins

Prenatal and Perinatal Psychology:
A New Way of Thinking About the Beginning of Life

Prenatal and Perinatal Psychology brings us some extraordinary new discoveries, based on the latest research, that are changing the way we think about pregnancy, birth, and the first few months of life. Below are seven principles that are helping us to shape the ways we treat young families and their babies.

Seven Principles of Prenatal and Perinatal Psychology

1. Conception, pregnancy, and birth are natural processes.

2. Pregnant mothers and babies share experiences.

3. Babies are conscious, aware and expressive—talking, playing, breathing, posture, sounds, movement.

4. Babies need loving support for optimal development.

5. Babies' first relationships lay the foundation for all future relationships (in the womb, feeling wanted, supported, protected from stress, and emotionally volatile relationships).

6. Experience dramatically affects the development of babies' brains.

7. Imprints from early experiences can be enhanced or transformed at any time.

Notes:

♥ For a mother to be able to nurture her baby, she needs to be fully supported by those around her.

♥ Connections in the brain are being formed even before birth. All experiences play a part in shaping the brain.

♥ Feel the oneness with your baby.

♥ Imagine baby's movement, sound, breathing rhythm, and heart rhythm as your baby communicating.

♥ When your baby starts to cry, he/she will be soothed and often stop crying if the mother will pick up the baby within 90 seconds.

Note: Prepared by Dr. Marti Glenn and Jamie Suard of Santa Barbara Graduate Institute, Department of Prenatal and Perinatal Psychology, in collaboration with Newmark Management Institute, *The Children's Project.* (For written materials and DVDs on how our earliest life experiences profoundly shape the quality of our lives, and information about graduate courses of study, contact the Institute by e-mail at: info@sbgi.edu.) Some examples highly recommended by the Institute are:

Takikawa, D., *What Babies Want: An Exploration of the Consciousness of Infants,* DVD. Los Olivos, CA: Hana Peace Works, 2004.

This heartwarming film brings together groundbreaking information about what babies truly are, what they know, and how we can support them to be their best as they develop and grow. Narrated by Noah Wiley.
(www.whatbabieswant.com)

Takikawa, D., *Wondrous Beginnings: An Audio Interview with Wendy Anne McCarty, PhD,* Audio CD. Los Olivos, CA: Hana Peace Works, 2007.

A leader in the field of prenatal and perinatal psychology is interviewed and helps people to enter into a new way of perceiving a baby as an aware being who has the capacity to understand, to relate, and to have meaningful communication.
(www.whatbabieswant.com
and www.wondrousbeginnings.com)

McCarty, W. A., *Being with Babies: What Babies Are Teaching Us,* Vols. I & II. Santa Barbara, CA: Wondrous Beginnings Publishing, 2000.

These booklets distill new principles and recommendations to support babies from clinical research with babies that reveal new levels of awareness and communication from the beginning of life.
(www.wondrousbeginnings.com)

Role of Secondary Education in a Democratic and Changing Society

Secondary education (high school) occupies that portion of a person's life which may be characterized as the period of transition from adolescence to adulthood. Becoming an adult signifies taking more responsibility for one's own life, making more decisions on one's own (especially significant personal decisions concerning work, recreation, education, and relations with the opposite sex), becoming self-supporting financially, and generally moving from dependency to independence. It also should mean assuming more responsibility for improving the quality of life in the community and becoming a more active participant in the democratic processes of society.

Secondary education, therefore, is in the business of "growing adults." In doing so, it must consider the needs of the individual and of the community. Adolescents need to explore, have choices, develop interests, and achieve confidence, competence, and a sense of self-worth. The community needs individuals of integrity who are cooperative, caring, and civic-minded.

One of the problems in achieving an effective transition from adolescence to adulthood has been the relative isolation and segregation of the young from adult activities. Another has been the constraints inherent in confining education to the schoolhouse and in the traditional structure of large group, lock-step instruction with the teacher as the sole disseminator of information and the student as the passive recipient. Further, the hierarchical, autocratic nature of most schools has created adversarial rather than cooperative relations among school participants. Instead of the school being the most interesting and exciting environment in every community, too often students, teachers, and administrators are bored, frustrated, unhappy, or angry.

To "grow adults," the school itself must grow up. The secondary school must become a learning community with its various members joined in a common effort to improve the learning of all. Graduates of this type of community should be recognized by their capability for self-directed study; ability to work cooperatively and effectively with peers; positive attitudes toward learning; high levels of competence in selected areas of the curriculum; confidence in their ability to learn new things; concern for the growth, development and well-being of others; and readiness to succeed in higher education or in the work force.

Major Goal Areas

ACQUISITION OF KNOWLEDGE AND SKILLS

Secondary education should assist students in acquiring the knowledge and skills necessary to function effectively in society and to understand and enjoy the world about them. By age 18, every student should have developed competence in the basic communication skills of listening, speaking, reading, and writing. Since these basic skills are essential to continuing one's education, to entering the work world, and to effective citizenship, these skills should receive attention in conjunction with teaching the subject matter of every course.

Students who desire to go on to higher education will follow a prescribed program to meet college entrance requirements, but they also should have the opportunity to choose one academic subject in which to achieve special competence. Those students who do not intend to go to college should have the opportunity to develop proficiency in an occupation that may be filled by a high-school graduate. He should be equipped to begin earning a living on a part-time or full-time basis upon graduation. All students should be encouraged to seriously consider the college option. A change along the way in either direction should be facilitated after receiving guidance from a parent and counselor.

Ideally, every student should engage in some individual sport which could provide lifelong exercise and enjoyment. And, in addition to developing an appreciation for good health, each student should plan and participate in an individual exercise program. Every student should be encouraged to develop appreciation for art and music and be provided with an opportunity to become proficient in some aspect of either.

One of the most important, rewarding, and perhaps most difficult areas of life is that of relationships with the opposite sex. Yet, students have little preparation for courtship, sexual relations, marriage, or parenthood. Opportunities to question, study, learn, and discuss should be provided throughout secondary education.

CAPABILITY FOR SELF-DIRECTED LEARNING

In the age of "future shock," everything changes constantly and the only constant is change itself. New information becomes dated or obsolete almost as fast as it is discovered. Technological advances often carry with them the seed of future problems. Effective functioning requires the ability to learn continually throughout one's life. Under these conditions, self-directed learning is an important educational objective. The self-directed learner is able to formulate his own goals, consider alternatives, prepare a plan, choose and utilize material and human resources effectively, evaluate his own progress, revise plans, work at a task independently, and persist long enough to bring them to fruition. The Internet provides innumerable opportunities to support such activities, and schools should encourage its use.

INTERPERSONAL RELATIONS AND A SENSE OF COMMUNITY

Our society has tremendous problems as witnessed by ever-increasing school dropouts, vandalism, divorce rates, drug abuse, crime and violence in the streets, dishonesty in government, race relations—and war, war, war. Adversary relations and conflicts exist at all levels in our present world—village, town, city, state, nation, and international—plus let's not forget parent-child, marital, and family relations. Most of our problems are not technical problems but are people problems. We do not seem to be able to get along with each other, to trust, to communicate, to care, to work together. People helping people is no longer a luxury but a matter of survival.

Secondary education should develop skills in working cooperatively with others, in developing a sense of ownership in our institutions, and in creating positive environments where people treat people in emotionally healthy ways. The school should become a learning community with each classroom a micro-community.

Methodology

INDIVIDUALIZED INSTRUCTION

The ratio of one teacher to 30 or more students makes it almost impossible to attend to the wide range of individual differences in aptitude, abilities, motivation, learning styles, and achievement levels. Material and methods should allow each student to progress at his or her own pace, receive individual help when, where, and how he needs it. These have been available for some time in the form of cross-age student tutoring, programmed instruction, computer-assisted learning, and other self-teaching material; smaller class size; volunteers in the classroom; and big brother and mentor programs. Nevertheless, their implementation in schools across the nation has not been widespread or consistent.

STUDENT TUTORING

Learning by teaching, or peer and cross-age student tutoring, is an important method of individualizing instruction and is also highly motivating. As a recipient, the student receives individual help; as a tutor, the student sharpens his own learning skills.

Secondary education should promote the broad notion of the helping relationship within every classroom and across grade levels. This is not a remedial approach, but rather one in which all students become resources for one another by working in teams. Everyone learns to teach and teaches to learn.

Student tutoring helps develop a sense of community, caring, and responsibility. Being placed in a position of responsibility motivates the tutor and makes him feel important. Assisting other children to learn helps him test, develop, and internalize his own knowledge. It gives the tutor insights into the learning process. Competition is replaced by cooperation.

SHARED PLANNING AND DECISION MAKING

Our nation prides itself in its democratic institutions, yet we attempt to prepare young people for active participation as citizens without offering them adequate opportunity to learn and practice the necessary skills. The secondary school should be a vibrant, living-learning community, where students develop a sense of ownership by participating in governing the school. Students, parents, and staff should jointly establish goals and plans and carry them out. As students develop a sense of proprietorship, absenteeism, dropouts, underachieving, and apathy will decrease and be replaced by interest, excitement, participation, caring, and concern. Students become turned on to school and to one another.

TASK-ORIENTED FEEDBACK

No matter how much cohesiveness exists at the outset among professional practitioners (teachers and administrators) and the clients (children and parents), conflicts will appear, especially as circumstances change. The test of character of any organization or community is not the absence of differences and conflicts but rather how these are handled. Mishandled, they become destructive to the educational process. Handled well, they become a positive force for effective change. Thus, the school must have built-in provisions for self-criticism and self-correction. The task-oriented feedback session is such a mechanism.

Task-oriented group feedback is an opportunity through regular, open discussion to understand the effects one's actions have on others and vice versa. It is a time when people can share problems, and ask for and offer help. It is an exercise in self-government where all decisions and actions can be questioned, including those of persons in authority. It is an occasion to share views honestly, in a non-threatening atmosphere, a place where people learn how not to respond defensively to criticism but to welcome it as a means of learning and clearing the air.

Feedback sessions are generally unstructured and without any agenda. The basic question addressed is: "What do we see each other doing, or ourselves, that is either hindering or helping us achieve the school's objectives and maintain a high morale?"

COMMUNITY AS A CLASSROOM

A major problem mentioned in achieving an effective transition from adolescence to adulthood is the relative isolation of the young from important adult activities. One of the ways of changing this is through the concept of the "community as a classroom."

This concept emphasizes that all the people, places, and events of the community at large represent potentially rich and important resources for learning that can and should be systematically exploited. The "Yellow Pages of Learning Resources," Group for Environmental Education, Inc., Philadelphia, 1972, a manual concerned with the potential of the city as a place for learning, states: "Education has been thought of as taking place mainly within the confines of the classroom, and school buildings have been regarded as the citadels of knowledge. However, the most extensive facility imaginable for learning is our urban environment. It is a classroom without walls, an open university for people of all ages offering a boundless curriculum with unlimited expertise. If we can make our urban environment comprehensible and observable, we will have created classrooms with endless windows on the world."

As the city becomes a classroom, and the skills and knowledge of parents and community people are brought into the classroom and school on a regular basis to give lectures, workshops, and demonstrations, the isolation of youth will be broken. Knowledge and motivation will be enhanced as students hear from these real-world role models.

Summing Up

An important reason that schools are failing—and even the most successful are underachieving—is the lack of a sense of community and a feeling of powerlessness. Money, materials, equipment, and new buildings, while important and necessary, will have limited impact on results as long as children, parents, teachers, and administrators feel powerless and experience themselves as victims or adversaries. The school must have a cohesive philosophy and program around which enthusiasm, energy, and support can be mobilized.

The secondary school should attempt to become a "learning community," characterized by the feeling that problems are "our problems," failures are "our failures," and successes are "our successes." This is based on the idea that people learn, grow, participate, and contribute best in a situation where they feel they have some control over their own destinies.

Students should acquire intellectual and vocational competence, a sense of self-worth, the ability to learn on their own, concern for the well-being of others, and skill in working cooperatively. This should enable students to face the future with confidence and excitement, whether they continue their formal education or enter the world of work.

Acknowledgments

*M*y sincere gratitude goes to the children, parents, and teachers of Wilshire Crest, Dublin Ave., and Pacoima elementary schools in Los Angeles—all participants in the Tutorial Community Project where the idea for this book first originated. They taught me a great deal about parent-child-teacher relations.

My thanks to a number of people who critiqued the first edition. Their comments and suggestions improved the final document. They were: Jan Amsterdam, Kaela Austin, Kathy Cohen, Bill Crawford, Terry David, Denis Girard, Shirley Kessler, Trisha King, Dr. Fred Penrose, Richard Satzman, Dr. Harry Silberman. My thanks also to Nina Rosenfield and Mitzi Thaler who contributed to the second edition. Some individuals provided advice, ideas, and encouragement throughout the project. Their contributions significantly improved the final product and were personally and professionally gratifying to me. They were: Steve Gussman, Dr. Richard Helfant, Dr. Ralph Melaragno; also, making special contributions to both editions were: Don Friese, Dr. Peter Huber, Marian Schiff, Dan Stein, and Gail Zeserman.

I am indebted also to Alfredo Tarin, Principal of Reseda High School (CA), for his insights into the importance of emotional health in school and in life. His leadership efforts to create an emotional-health-friendly school culture included encouraging teachers to employ emotional health concepts in the classroom, parents to participate in parent support groups, and students in parent-child relations seminars. Within this program, thanks also to Rosalva Waterford, Parent Center Director, for supervising parent support groups, to Heather Sardella for facilitating these groups, Brigit Diaz for helping to make the participation of ninth-grade students a valuable experience, and to Elba Bugarin and Marianne Maki for coordinating the ninth-grade project.

Thanks to Stan Corwin, my agent, for his advice and belief in the book, and to Evelyne Duval, my international agent, for her success in having the book published in several foreign countries. My appreciation to Aviva Layton, whose careful editing of both editions added much to the clarity and conciseness of each book. Thanks also to Frieda Greene and Cynthia Citron for their careful proofreading. Kathy Arft's help in gathering information, checking on details, and typing final drafts for both editions were much appreciated. Special thanks to Steve Gussman for the cover design and as always for his emphasis on getting it right. Many thanks to Tina Hill for her book design and computer typesetting, and also for her patience and positive attitude in dealing with last-minute changes for both editions.

I am very grateful to Dr. Alex Kopelowitz for his book critique and personal counsel during periods of stress. Dr. Fran Kahn helped me stay level-headed and focused at times when I was tempted to go off in different directions. For that, and her ongoing support and encouragement, I am deeply grateful. My gratitude also to Dr. Giovanni Aponte and the Meadowbrook staff for their support and dedication. And to Norman Horowitz, thanks for your friendship, advice, and provocative ideas. Thanks to Ken Ng for his hand-eye coordination and sense of humor—one or both of which has kept me in good condition and spirits. Thanks to Karen West for her lively personality and commitment to keeping me on my toes. Numerous and lengthy conversations with Patricia Sun on parenting were inspirational and invaluable. My love to my mother-in-law, Annie Zeserman, for who she is and for bringing Deborah into this world. And thanks to my boyhood friends from P.S. 96, P.S. 89, and Columbus High in the Bronx who gave me a sense of community during a childhood that was frequently "trying" but also exhilarating.

To my older, better-looking, richer, smarter, and occasionally wiser brother, Irv, thanks for the years of conversation about parenting, where we could identify aspects of our behavior that did not always enhance the emotional health of our children. Also, thanks for your constant love and support which have always been important to me.

To my mother and father, Esther and Joe, my eternal thanks for leaving me with such positive feelings about the importance of family.

Finally to my son, David, my heartfelt gratitude for teaching me important lessons about patience, perseverance, understanding, courage, and love in a way that no one else could.

This edition was published with financial support from the Center for ReUniting Families. We greatly appreciate this contribution to further our efforts on behalf of parents, children, families, and schools.

About the Author

GERALD NEWMARK, Ph.D., president of the Newmark Management Institute, is a parent, educator, researcher, and management consultant. Throughout his career, Dr. Newmark has employed a combination of common sense and scientific method to help organizations and individuals become more effective.

For 15 years, he was a research scientist, first with the Rand Corporation, System Development Division, and later with the System Development Corporation, where his work focused on the design, development, and evaluation of innovative training and instructional systems for public schools and military programs.

Under a seven-year Ford Foundation grant, Dr. Newmark worked with children, parents, and teachers in Los Angeles city schools as co-director of a project to develop a model school. The results of this effort are described in his book, *This School Belongs to You and Me: Every Learner a Teacher, Every Teacher a Learner.* For this work, Dr. Newmark received a presidential citation.

An important aspect of Dr. Newmark's adult life has been participation in civic and youth affairs. He was involved for six years with the Synanon Foundation in its pioneering work in the treatment of drug addiction, and with Operation Bootstrap in Central Los Angeles in projects to improve interracial relations. He has been a consultant to the California Special Olympics and the California State Department of Education. Dr. Newmark has served on the advisory boards of the National Commission on Resources for Youth, the Center for ReUniting Families, and two drug abuse programs—Amity, Inc., in Arizona, and Tuum Est (now Phoenix House) in Los Angeles. He presently serves on the Board of Directors of the Catticus Corporation, a non-profit organization producing educational media for public radio and TV.

Dr. Newmark is a member of the American Association of Humanistic Psychology, the Charles F. Menninger Society, and the National Association for the Mentally Ill.